"This book is essential reading for anyone who wants to create a career they love."
- **Peter Cook**, CEO of Thought Leaders

"The most successful people are highly passionate about their vocation, and that passion becomes contagious in their working environment. I've known Rachel for 15 years, and you won't meet a more passionate person dedicated to helping people maximize their potential. Focus on what Rachel is providing you, as it will change your working life!"
- **Jamie Shanks**, CEO, Sales for Life Canada

"This book is a must for anyone who feels they aren't reaching their true potential"
- **Colette Werden**, Authentic Personal Branding Expert

"This book is an essential for anyone who wants to reach their full potential"
- **Alex Pirouz**, Founder of Linkfluencer

WORK IT REAL GOOD

HOW TO FIND AND DO WORK YOU LOVE

FOREWORD BY LUCY FEAGINS; EDITOR OF THE DESIGN FILES
- AUSTRALIA'S MOST POPULAR DESIGN BLOG

BY RACHEL SPARKES

First published 2016 by

by Lulu Publishers

© Text and Images Rachel Sparkes 2016

All rights reserved. No part of this publication may be reproduced, stored in a retrieval system, or transmitted in any form by any means (electronic, mechanical, photocopying, recording or otherwise) without prior written permission of the publisher.

National Library of Australia Cataloguing-in-Publication data:

Creator: Sparkes, Rachel.

Title: Work It Real Good: How to Find and Do Work You Love by Rachel Sparkes

ISBN: 978-1-326-85625-0

Notes: Includes index.

Subjects: Career Transformation
Personal Development
Personal Transformation

Cover Design, Typeset, Illustrations & Diagrams by: Linden Duck

Edited by Debra Hilton and Jo Stewart.

Printed in Australia by Lulu Publishers

Printed on demand worldwide by Lulu Publishers.

CONTENTS

Acknowledgements
About the Author
Foreword by Lucy Feagins

PART 1 - THE CONSCIOUS CAREER
Chapter 1 - Introduction — 1
Chapter 2 - Factors Affecting Todays Workplace — 11
Chapter 3 - Top 10 Career Mistakes — 25

PART 2 - THE EPIC CAREER QUEST
Chapter 4 - The Decision Dial — 33
Chapter 5 - Passion and Purpose — 39
Chapter 6 - Heart-Mind Connection — 45

PART 3 - THE CAREER COMPASS
Chapter 7 – The Career Navigators Roadmap — 59

The Deliver-IT Quadrant
Chapter 8 – Your Achievement — 67
Chapter 9 – Your Attitude — 69
Chapter 10 – Your Awareness — 73

The Discover-IT Quadrant
Chapter 11 – Your Identity — 79
Chapter 12 – Your Influences — 93
Chapter 13 – Your Interests — 103

The Design-IT Quadrant
Chapter 14 – Your Goals — 113
Chapter 15 – Your Gaps — 119
Chapter 16 – Your Game Plan — 131

The Do-IT Quadrant
Chapter 17 – Your Power — 135
Chapter 18 – Your Positioning — 141
Chapter 19 - Your Promotion — 145

Chapter 20 - Your Journey — 167

ACKNOWLEDGEMENTS

This journey and this book would not have been possible without the Thought Leaders Business School or the endless support of my former partner and father of my beautiful son Max - James O'Dea. I will always be grateful for your patience and support and belief in me.

To my family - Nicole Sparkes you are my rock, my inspiration and my sounding board for all things in life and business thank you. To my mother, Jill Sparkes - thank you for your help and support with family and inside the business. To my dad Rex Sparkes and step-mum Deb Sparkes - your positive support and consistent thoughtfulness is deeply appreciated. To my sister Joy, your kindness and good heart and support is deeply appreciated. And to my brother Keith Sparkes, who left us too young - I know you would be proud of this book and are looking down on this with a big 'Keefy' grin. To my Aunt Chrissy - thank you for telling me to 'stop spinning my wheels and just do something' when I was 20 and always being an inspiration to me. To my cousin Lucy for following and taking action on her dreams thank you - you are an inspiration to me. To Jennifer O'Dea who is also the best mother-in-law that a girl could have asked for and grandmother a boy could ask for. Your support and encouragement is appreciated thank you.

To my mentors Georgia Murch, Alex Pirouz, Mark Middo, Pete Cook, Matt Church, Dermott Crowley, Ben Cordeiro, Jon Sampson, George Skordos and the many more individuals who have problem solved, ideated and guided me over the years thank you!

To my beautiful friends who inspire me and accept me for who I am and believe in me and allow me to incessantly talk about 'work' and test my 'stuff' on them all the time: Catherine Evans - you are an earth angel, Andy Evans - I love you like a brother, Cadi Staton - you are the truest friend with the most amazing heart, to Laryssa Johnston - my first #mumrock I wouldn't have made it through the first year of motherhood without you. You're an inspiration to working mothers everywhere and you have taught me the healing power of forgiveness.

The entire Albert Park mothers group; Fiona, Caroline, Penny and Nia thanks for listening to my ideas over the years. To the school #mumsquad Nadine, Jo, Liv, Clare, Marina, Soula, Tania and Sarah thanks for the last minute play dates and drop'n run parties when I've had to dash away for work.

To my oldest friends; Jessica and Bart Simes, Nicole Thompson, Bec Whiting, Belza Frith, Kristy Keyte, Michael Stunden, Simone Donovan, Jamie Shanks, Nicole Dickmann, Bianca Oheme, Alicia Kimber, Kerry Sanders and Pip Varley thank you for always believing in me and supporting me over the many iterations of my career and businesses over the years!

And of course, to those involved in this project; my editor Jo Stewart and graphic designer and book designer Linden Duck! Without you two this book would not be what it is. I'm so fortunate to have worked with such talented and passionate people. Thank you!

- Rachel Sparkes

ABOUT THE AUTHOR

Rachel Sparkes is *"Australia's Leading Career Transformation Expert"* according to Huffington Post. She has spent the last 15 years in the careers industry including running her own IT Recruitment Agency, HR Consultancy for the software industry and International Career Transformation Coaching business.

Originally from Adelaide she now lives in Melbourne, Australia with her son. She is a true multi-potentialite with a passion for TV presenting, digital marketing, conscious music, poetry and song-writing as well as a dedicated practice of yoga and meditation.

She is the founder of Rachel Sparkes International and the online career and business coaching platform - **The IP3 Academy: Unlocking Individual Performance, Purpose and Potential in the Workplace**. You can learn more about her and her business and programs at www.rachelsparkes.com.au

FOREWORD

There are people whose greatest dreams and aspirations rely on a fantasy of not having to work. These people go through life essentially planning for retirement. 'One day, I'll stop working, sell my house and sail the world', 'One day, when I don't have to work anymore, I'll finally be able to write that screenplay I always dreamed of writing'.

How depressing.

Do we really have to wait until we're retired to be fulfilled in life?

In fact, I believe the opposite is true. I believe being incredibly busy is the greatest joy in life. Waiting years until you have nothing left to do is the most depressing way to waste away a lifetime. There is nothing to be enjoyed in doing nothing - really, there isn't. Life is finite, after all, and every last second should be savoured!

The key, of course, is to seek out the right kind of busy.

In this book, careers expert Rachel Sparkes makes an impassioned case for finding and doing the work you love. Because a joyful life isn't about escaping work, or circumventing the need to work - it's about filling each day to the brim, with work that is so inspiring, so much fun and so truly enriching, that it doesn't feel like work at all.

If we're lucky, each of us has 28,000 days on this Earth, and it's our choice how we will fill them. Don't squander your days. Don't waste a minute. Make sure each day is brilliantly busy.

Lucy x

LUCY FEAGINS
Editor - THE DESIGN FILES

PART I

THE CONSCIOUS CAREER

CHAPTER 1
INTRODUCTION

> *"The secret of finding and doing the work you love is not about achievement in itself. It's ultimately about being fully self-aware and self-expressed. It's about realising you're pure potentiality and that your potential is limitless and never stops growing or desiring to be expressed. It is always about the journey - not the destination."*
>
> *-Rachel Sparkes*

If you are reading this book you probably fall into one of five camps:

1. You're satisfied with your career but want to know how to stand out in your work place so you can accelerate your path to greater satisfaction and success.

2. You're totally unhappy with your current career trajectory and want a complete career overhaul.

3. You're at a crossroads in your career, feeling a sense of unease but aren't able to identify the root of the problem.

4. You may be a school-leaver or College/University graduate entering the corporate world for the first time looking for a 'heads up' on how the whole game is played.

5. You have had a career break (voluntary or not) and are re-thinking your career and next steps, but not exactly sure how to go about it.

I love to ask kids what they want to be when they grow up. You get the most interesting answers. They say things like: fire-fighter, nurse, teacher, doctor, and professional skateboarder! When you ask high school students the same question, their ideas are still generally pretty cool: documentary filmmaker, traveller, entrepreneur, actor...

I don't know about you, but when I imagined attending my 10 or 20 year school reunion, I always thought that I would be doing something extraordinarily amazing in my career and that all my dreams of happiness and fulfilment would have come true. The problem is that when I talk to people in their late 30s and 40s many of them are not experiencing that level of fulfilment or happiness.

They say things like:

- I've 'checked-out' of my job and I'm feeling unhappy...
- I feel stuck at a certain level and can't seem to move forward...
- All I do is 'give' to the company...
- I feel burnt-out...
- I feel insecure in my career...
- I don't feel like my true self in my career...
- I'm just going through the motions at work...
- I have no idea what I want to do with my career...
- I feel like there is something (or someone) holding me back from doing what I really want...
- I feel overwhelmed and stressed all of the time...

These are people who have senior level roles, big salaries, company cars and company credit cards. They've bought large homes and are sending their kids to expensive private schools, but as they look around they are asking: 'Is this all there is?'

THE REAL PROBLEM

The real problem underneath all of these other ones is simple. Fear. We are so afraid of not being good enough, of what others think of us. We have so many fears that we don't end up living our full potential.

Introduction

So what if I told you I could take you from fear and frustration, to freedom and flow in your career?

THE SIX STAGES OF CAREER TRANSFORMATION

After working with thousands of people who were mostly looking to find more money, satisfaction or stability in their careers, I found that there are six clear stages of 'career transformation'. Take a look at the graph below and think about where you might be right now.

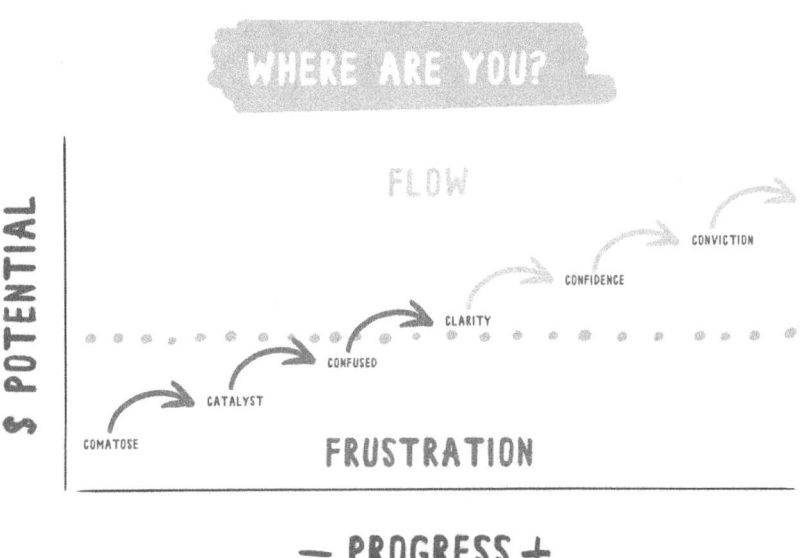

So imagine that the 'Progress' axis represents movement in your career. It's your positional moves, your personal development and ability to get things done in your current role. The left hand side represents minimal progress and the right hand side represents a lot of progress in these areas. The 'Potential' axis encapsulates not only your earning potential but your potential to grow your talents, do your best work, be fulfilled and feel a sense of purpose. Again the bottom end represents low potential and the upper end represents high potential.

What happens is that most people who come to see me are in a state of frustration, and there are three stages of this.

The first stage is **COMATOSE**. In this stage you may be doing nothing about your career or not realising that anything needs to be done. You are blissfully unaware and pretty much reactive. You only act when you have to or if you start to feel unhappy. You'll notice that both the 'Potential' and 'Progress' axes in the Comatose phase are pretty limited in this stage.

The second stage is **CATALYST**. This is when something happens to you to snap you awake. You realise you need to do something about your career. Either a redundancy, horrible boss, family crisis, health issue or even that nagging feeling that won't go away forces you to do something about your career.

The third stage is **CONFUSION**. You know you need to do something but where on earth do you start? You are unsure what is right for you or perhaps how to go about your career planning in a strategic manner. It may all seem too overwhelming on top of your busy work schedule and commitments.

All of these three stages are characterised by frustration, stagnation and confusion. But underneath all of this is a sense of self-doubt that perhaps you can't do what you love and get paid good money to do it. Well you can! In my work as a career navigator and business coach, I've seen many success stories of people going through this stage, then flourishing beyond their dreams. This book is going to help you do this also. It's called getting into 'Flow'.

There are three steps to getting into flow in your career.

The first is **CLARITY**. This is when you take the time to discover what is at the heart of your career motivations and needs. You get clear on your influences, values, strengths, interests and desires for the future. Essentially, you identify what you want.

The second step is **CONFIDENCE**. In this stage you identify how to get where you want to go in clear, actionable steps. You use your clarity to design your goals and make an emotional connection to the people and path that will help you get there. By the end of this stage you now know how to get where you want to go.

The third step is **CONVICTION**. The ultimate career destination is working in full alignment with your 'personal why', otherwise known as your purpose. It's working with people you like, doing work that satisfies you, getting paid what you're worth, in a way that works for you. In this stage, you know why you do what you do.

When you have your What, How and Why in alignment, you are in a state of flow and you are able to do your best work. Your earning potential goes through the roof, you make incredible progress in your career and you feel fulfilled and energised. This is what an epic career is all about and what this book is designed to help you achieve.

A CORPORATE CATASTROPHE

After university, I became an IT Recruitment expert. I steadily moved up through the ranks, confident that security and financial stability were absolutely mine. I was doing extremely well, and joined an IT Recruitment company which was on BRW's Fastest 100 list. In 2007, I was invited to become a part-owner in this company which I loved. I loved the people I worked with and the culture we had created. Using a combination of my savings and a loan of $50,000, I invested $100,000 in this company anticipating that within a few years I would have made it all back tenfold. Only a year later the Global Financial Crisis (GFC) hit and the company went into receivership. I was on maternity leave at the time, and was left with no job, no savings, and a massive bank debt. When that company closed, I lost far more than the money I had invested, I lost a part of my heart in the process. This was one of the darkest times of my career and life.

I worked for a large recruitment firm for about a year to get back on my feet, then in 2011 I started my own IT Recruitment company in Melbourne, Australia. I was going to re-create that utopia, but this time I would have total control. I quickly hired staff, won some impressive clients and things were going really well. I bought a brand new BMW, shopped at Louis Vuitton and had a wardrobe of designer clothes. I was able to purchase a house in the suburb I wanted and pay for the glamorous wedding of my dreams. However, something had changed. At night I'd hear this little voice whispering, "Is this all there is? What's it all for?" I desperately wanted to ignore that little voice because I was 'doing everything I wanted to do' but it just wouldn't leave me.

After a year or so things went from good to not so good in the business. I had some issues with key staff, then I lost 90% of my business when two key accounts left. I was soon in a position where I had to reconsider my entire business model and decide if I wanted to be in the business at all. It was an enormously stressful time and again I was left wondering, "What am I doing this for?"

MY AWAKENING

I didn't realise it for many years, but like many others my career choices were formed early in life by incidents that were relatively trivial. I was raised in suburban Adelaide by working class parents: my father; a thoughtful, loving, hard working 'big kid' and my mother - a courageous, competent and highly intelligent woman who separated when I was about 15 years old. I remember going to the grocery store with mum one day, shortly after dad had moved out and when we got to the checkout, her payment wouldn't process. She tried two or three cards that day but there was no money in the accounts and we had to put the groceries back. I never found out what went wrong, and it never happened again, but the humiliation and distress we both felt that day led me to vow that never again would I not have enough money to pay for groceries. Part of my own awakening was realising the influence emotional events like this had on my career. That one belief drove me to make my career choices based on security and remuneration.

WHAT IS MY LIFE ALL ABOUT?

Around the same time I had this 'awakening' I suffered a miscarriage. I was devastated and felt somewhere inside that it was the result of all the stress and anxiety that I was living through each day. It was then that I knew I had to stop and listen to what my heart and body were trying to tell me. I made the decision to let all my staff go and reconsider my entire career journey. This was the catalyst I needed to stop travelling mindlessly onwards, and to start listening to my inner voice again.

I went to yoga to heal and after about a year and a half of doing yoga with the firm intention of 'listening' to what my career direction should be, one day it hit me. I was no longer satisfied with recruitment or just making money for my own personal gain. Something had changed in me and I wanted more meaning, purpose and fulfilment in the work I was doing. I wanted to be real and to be 100% passionate and purpose-driven and I just couldn't see how to do that in the recruitment game.

Shortly after this, I had another revelation: Career Coaching was where I fit! I could hardly believe how loud and clear this idea was. There was no mistaking my inner voice. In his book *The Way of the Peaceful Warrior*, by Dan Millman talks about tapping into his intuition through meditation. He says that when he heard his inner voice speak to him it was definitely different from a passing thought, it was a voice that was clearly guiding him, like a message from his higher self. That's what this felt like. It was so clear and so obvious that I almost leapt off the mat in that moment and rushed home to implement my new plan.

Introduction

THE OBVIOUS CHOICE

It sounds simple, but when I started to talk to friends and colleagues about my new career idea I discovered that many of them were experiencing the same problems. As I shared the tools I had developed to guide my own search for a career I loved with them and saw them taking control of their life and work choices, I realised that that was what I really wanted to do with my life: help people find careers they love And so, in 2013 my Career Navigation business was born. I called it *'I Heart My Job'*.

WOULD YOU LIKE TO LEARN HOW TO FIND WORK YOU LOVE?

Of course you would! I've talked to (a few) people who didn't think it was possible. They believed that work was work and just had to be endured so you could pay the bills and feed yourself and your family. These people wouldn't believe that anything could be different, ro matter what they did. However, most people say, "Yes!" when I ask this question. Their problem is, "How can I do this?" This book will help you answer that question and provide a clear roadmap to help you get from wherever you are now, to an emphatic, "I love my job!"

Along the way, you'll have to do some hard thinking, and it may take some time to develop the skills and make the changes you need, but you'll have a clear picture of where this work is taking you that will make it all worthwhile.

WHAT THIS BOOK WILL TEACH YOU

The way to work with this book is to read it from beginning to end at least once. That way you will get the big picture ideas of career transformation, potentiality and listening to your own inner guidance at first glance. Then depending on what you need - a complete career overhaul or just specific guidance – you can move to the sections that serve you.

As you read this book, you will discover that you can determine your own career path and that you have the power to choose a career that makes your heart light up. I like to call this The Conscious Career. This is what Part One is all about and designed to bring you to a place of total personal awareness about your current career.

Featuring in Part Three of the book, the Career Navigators Roadmap is a step-by-step action plan to take anyone from Comatose to Convicted as explained in the introduction. It is a roadmap that is designed to get you doing work you love, with people you like, getting paid what you're worth, working in a way that suits you. But not everyone wants or is ready for complete career transformation - and that's cool. Perhaps you just want some clarity on today's work landscape or advice on salary negotiation. This book has that too. Take what you need but know that this book and I are here for you in the long run.

With the help of this book, you'll be able to take back the control that you may have ceded many years ago to family, friends, teachers, and other probably well-meaning people, who may have guided you onto wrong paths.

Further on in this book we'll look at what it takes to create the perfect career. You'll learn exactly what you need to know and do to align your career with your passions and values, and why that is so important and you'll create your own unique Career Blueprint. I like to call this The Epic Career because we should go big and hard and be fabulously awesome while working out how to overcome every obstacle that lies in your path and follow your plan until you are pursuing the career you designed.

In the final part of this book you will be guided by The Career Compass. This becomes the physical companion to your own inner guidance system (aka your intuition) and step-by-step Career Navigators Roadmap that you can come back to again and again in your career. You can use this system to completely transform your career or make little tweaks here and there. It's your adventure so choose what works for you!

Along the way you'll learn the practical skills you need to find hidden job opportunities, do well in interviews, reach others on social media, and negotiate your salary effectively. It's going to take commitment on your part to work through the exercises and face your fears. You may even need to make some courageous decisions or face disapproval from others. Most people do face opposition when they're trying to achieve their dreams, and that's a good thing because it helps you decide just how much you want them.

WILL YOUR JOURNEY LOOK JUST LIKE MINE?

Your journey will reflect your own personality, desires, dreams, and goals. You don't have to give up anything unless you want to.

Introduction

For example, minimising may not be an integral part of your Epic Career Quest - although it's been wonderful for me.

This book is about creating a deliberately designed, whole-hearted career that fills the nagging void in your heart. It is about designing a Conscious Career. My goal is to help you find your true career path, a career that resonates with who you are and gives you what you want, without going through everything I went through - in fact, my goal is to help you avoid much of the time and agony I had to go through to find the career that I love.

In just a few short years I've been able to help hundreds of people understand why they felt that their job was such a grind, and discover the path to a career and lifestyle they really love. It's been a wild ride, but I'm loving the sense of purpose I feel, and the knowledge that I've played a part in so many personal transformations. After all, we spend an enormous proportion of our life working, so why invest all that time and effort into something we don't love?

CHAPTER 2
FACTORS AFFECTING TODAY'S WORKPLACE

"To raise new questions, new possibilities, to regard old problems from a new angle, requires creative imagination and marks real advance in science."
- Albert Einstein

After interviewing 10,000 or so people in my career, I was alarmed to learn that most people are basically unhappy with their work. In fact, Gallup Institute and other studies suggest that 87% of the global workforce are disengaged because of bad leadership[1]. I believe that the problem is much broader than the leadership and interpersonal skills of managers. I believe it's because we are at a time in history where there are social, technological and economic factors that are allowing us to make anything happen if we really want to. In this unique time in history, the collision of opportunity and the overwhelm of possibility is causing a large number of people to feel disengaged at work, to lose heart in their career, and to reconsider what path is right for them, than ever before – simply because they are very confused. Before we get into clearing up the confusion – let's look at the factors that impact on today's workplace.

---

1. Gallup's State of Global Workforce Report http://www.gallup.com/services/178517/state-global-workplace.aspx

These factors are:

- Technological - e.g. Acceleration of technological development
- Sociological - e.g. The Mindfulness movement
- Economic - e.g. Modern business models and globalisation

These watershed factors could affect your career progression and even prevent you from having a positive experience when you engage with certain organisations as a potential employee, so we need to look at each of them in more depth.

TECHNOLOGICAL FACTORS AFFECTING YOUR CAREER

During the Industrial Revolution, artisan weavers were swept aside by the mechanical loom. Over the past 30 years the Digital Revolution has displaced many of the mid-skill jobs that underpinned 20th-century middle-class life[2]. Typists, ticket agents, bank tellers and many production-line jobs have been dispensed with, just as the weavers were. One recent study by academics at Oxford University suggests that 47% of today's jobs could be automated in the next two decades.

At the same time, the Digital Revolution is transforming the process of innovation itself. Thanks to off-the-shelf code from the internet and platforms like Amazon's cloud computing that host services, Apple's app store that provide distribution and Facebook that offers marketing, the number of digital start-ups has exploded.

Add to that the increasing desire for people to work remotely and the cost benefit for organisations to employ mobile workforces, we will soon be seeing more productivity and consumer products on mobile platforms than ever before. We will also see exponential growth in the technological revolution and if you are working you will want to ride this exciting wave of supersonic progress.

As a futurist and an optimist I see that many jobs will be displaced in the next 10-50 years but I anticipate with wonder and excitement the incredible things we are about to discover and create, and the problems we will solve as a human race. Now is the time to think about what your

---

[2]. *CIO Magazine Online* by Meredith Levenson March 7th 2014-08-27

role will be during the digital and technological revolution and how you can use this either as a platform or a medium to get your message and vision out there in the world. Just 100 years ago, only the elite were able to own manufacturing plants and create products. Today, anyone can manufacture things through organisations like Alibaba, so your product is just a click away. Or think about publishing. In the 1950s, if you wanted to write a book you would have to shop your manuscript around to publishers and hope and pray that you would get a deal. Now, you can self-publish on blogs and social media and build a following without spending a dime. You can also self-publish an actual book and not get lumped into the 'vanity publishing' box. One start-up I heard about is looking at creating 'kill free' meat! This is an amazing concept: using stem cells to create biologically edible protein without harming any living creature or causing environmental damage! All of these things are made possible by the rise of technology.

However, not all technological development will help you achieve your goals. There are some issues that may affect your job search that you should be aware of. Some include:

APPLICANT TRACKING SYSTEMS (ATS)

Did you know that 'error-prone applicant tracking systems' kill 75% of job seekers' chances of landing an interview as soon as they submit their resumes, no matter how qualified they may be?

In a test conducted last year, Bersin & Associates created a perfect resume for an ideal candidate for a clinical scientist position. The research firm matched the resume to the job description and submitted the resume to an applicant tracking system from Taleo, arguably the leading maker of these systems.

When Bersin & Associates studied how the resume rendered in the applicant tracking system, the company saw that one of the candidate's positions was lost entirely because the date was typed before the employer details. The applicant tracking system also failed to read several educational degrees the candidate held, which would have given a recruiter the impression that the candidate lacked the education necessary for the job. The end result: The resume Bersin & Associates submitted only scored a 43 percent relevance ranking for the job because the applicant tracking system misread it.

As a job seeker, this means that if you are only applying for jobs via online job postings you are abandoning your career to chance, and also exposing it to a lot of technological failure. In Part Two of this book you will learn effective techniques to get around application tracking systems.

If you are a leader or manager searching for top talent, you could be missing out on the best-qualified applicants if you are relying too heavily on your technology. This book will help you design talent experiences that ensure you attract high quality candidates who are aligned with your vision and values and will perform at the highest level.

THE RISE OF VIDEO AND VIRTUAL REALITY

Video resumes and video interviews (like Skype, Google Hangouts, Zoom, GoToMeeting) have become more common in today's technologically-savvy organisations. Three years ago when I asked people if they had ever had an interview on Skype almost 100% of them would say, "No, this is my first time." Now when I ask the question I get closer to a 50-50 response. People still prefer to meet face-to-face, but remote interviews are increasingly popular as they save travel time.

The next generation of video usage is the use of short videos for job advertisements and employment branding. New technology platforms like 'Video My Job' allows employers to take their job advertisement to the next level and interview the line manager, talk to key stakeholders and show the prospective employee the physical location of their role. It's like doing work experience and interacting with your prospective team members from afar. This is not only a game-changer for organisations who want to be recognised as the home for top talent, it's also a potential way of getting your brand out to prospective employers.

A SHIFT TO ONLINE LEARNING

People are busier than ever at work, effective training delivery demands more resources, yet at the same time there is a never-ending demand for new levels of skills and on-going learning in most professions. Salman Khan from the Khan Institute is leading the way with the school of thought that learning is done best when self-paced for the core content, and supplemented by group work for key breakthroughs and individualised support.

The shift to high quality, online, on-demand courses that provide genuine depth and enable participants to keep up with the latest developments is rapidly increasing as internet speeds and technology improve.

ROBOTICS AND ARTIFICIAL INTELLIGENCE

Did you know that robotics and artificial intelligence are already having an impact on the job market and will have a bigger impact in the future? The vast majority of respondents to the Future of the Internet survey anticipate that robotics and artificial intelligence will permeate wide segments of daily life by 2025. Of the 1896 expert respondents to the survey, almost half of them said they envisioned a future in which robots and digital agents have displaced significant numbers of both blue and white-collar workers. The good news is the other half of the experts who responded to this survey (52%) expect that technology will not displace more jobs than it creates by 2025. Phew! It is a bit of a 'crystal ball' prediction about AI and robots but I also have faith that human ingenuity will create new jobs, industries, and ways to make a living, just as it has been doing since the dawn of the Industrial Revolution (and for millennia before that).

SKILLS GLOBALISATION

The rise and rise of free-market work based websites such as 99Designs, Fiverr, and Freelance.com are testament to the fact that skills can be sourced and bought from anywhere in the world cheaply. This is both a huge opportunity, as it opens up your skills and services to a global market, and also a huge threat to the value of what you do. It will be especially important to focus on being a master at what you do, getting good at it, and serving a tribe of raving fans - whether you are in a job or working in your own business.

INSIDE MESSAGING COMMUNITIES

Since the invention of Instant Messenger by Microsoft in the 90s there have been many different iterations of inside or in-house messaging to keep employees in touch with each other on a private network. Whether it's old school like Instant Messenger or the new kid on the block like Slack, these tools benefit your career in two main ways:-

- As an employee you can get your problems solved faster by the people you need to get in touch with almost immediately. If you are specifically looking to position yourself for a promotion or for a future job opportunity you can also have immediate access to your positioning targets and people of influence outside email or social media. You are 'on the inside' so to speak and in immediate touch with the exact people you need.

- As a leader you can also use these messaging communities to communicate your vision and message quickly and effectively. You can reiterate and show how you align with the behaviours and values in your organisation multiple times a day without having to worry about social media trolls getting a hold of it. At the same time, you can also observe how prospective future leaders interact in these forums and learn more about them.

MOBILISATION

One of the key shifts of the last 10 years has been the mobilisation of the workforce and this is continuing at dizzying speed. The banking industry in Australia has developed the 'hot-desk' scenario and other industries are following suit. Staff benefit from greater flexibility and more work/life balance, and organisations benefit from huge cost savings on real estate and infrastructure costs, plus more innovation and collaboration as people move fluidly around the office.

The enabler is mobilisation via technology. Desktops and applications appear the same way no matter what device you login on. Single sign-on technology and excellent security have been the backbone of this infrastructure and technological workplace revolution.

For those who have jumped ship into consulting and contracting it has become so much easier since 2000 with the low cost of entry for laptops, and the plethora of Software as a Service (SaaS), and affordable cloud-based subscription software options.

As a consultant and the owner of a mobilised micro-business for the past six years I have been able to build my entire business infrastructure on a laptop and a multitude of SaaS software that I pay either a monthly or an annual subscription for. I have worked in shared office spaces, from home, and from cafes. I have even coached clients from the poolside in Bali!

Because of the rise of technology, I see the future of work as a place of choice. When people can become their own individual 'brands' and work any time, any place, and in any way they please, individuals will focus on the specific value they create for the people and companies they interact with, rather than engage via traditional employment contracts.

SOCIOLOGICAL FACTORS AFFECTING YOUR CAREER

THE MINDFULNESS MOVEMENT

If you speak to the HR teams of many small, medium and large organisations today you will probably find a mindfulness workshop, meditation class or yoga membership as primary offerings to their staff. The wide-held belief is that the benefits of mindfulness movement include reduced stress and anxiety and promotion of general well-being. These well-being benefits translate into a healthier workforce, less sick days, higher engagement and at times more innovation.

According to the American Psychological association the imperial data that supports the benefits of mindfulness for individuals in corporate companies include:[3]

- Stress reduction. There were 39 studies conducted that explored the use of mindfulness-based stress reduction. The findings suggest that mindfulness meditation shifts people's ability to use emotion regulation strategies in a way that enables them to experience emotion selectively, and that the emotions they experience may be processed differently in the brain.

- Boosts to working memory. One study documented the benefits of mindfulness meditation among a military group who participated in an eight-week mindfulness training, a non-meditating military group and a group of non-meditating civilians. Both military groups were in a highly stressful period before deployment. The researchers found that the non-meditating military group had decreased working memory capacity over time. Within the meditating military group, however, working memory capacity increased with meditation practice.

- Focus. Another study examined how mindfulness meditation affected participants' ability to focus attention and suppress distracting information. The researchers compared a group of experienced mindfulness meditators with a control group that had no meditation experience. They found that the meditation group had significantly better performance on all measures of attention.

---

3. http://www.pewinternet.org/2014/08/06/future-of-jobs

- Less emotional reactivity. In a study of people who had anywhere from one month to 29 years of mindfulness meditation practice, researchers found that mindfulness meditation practice helped people disengage from emotionally upsetting pictures and enabled them to focus better on a cognitive task as compared with people who saw the pictures but did not meditate.

- Relationship satisfaction. The ability to respond well to relationship stress and the skill in communicating one's emotions to a partner. Empirical evidence suggests that mindfulness protects against the emotionally stressful effects of relationship conflict, is positively associated with the ability to express oneself in various social situations and predicts relationship satisfaction.

- Other benefits. Mindfulness has been shown to enhance self insight, morality, intuition and fear modulation, all functions associated with the brain's middle prefrontal lobe area. Evidence also suggests that mindfulness meditation has numerous health benefits, including increased immune functioning, improvement to well-being and reduction in psychological distress. In addition, mindfulness meditation practice appears to increase information processing, as well as decrease task effort and having thoughts that are unrelated to the task at hand.

So if you didn't think mindfulness, meditation or yoga was a good idea before – perhaps it's time to get your ommm on!

PERSONAL ALIGNMENT OF WORK

> "When you align your personal why with the organisation why, magic happens"
> - Rachel Sparkes

One of the best TED Talks of recent times is Simon Sinek's "Start With Why". He talks through this simple yet profound model that explains the shift of purpose in inspired organisations. His theory is that when organisations consider their purpose (why?) first, and then think about their delivery methods second, and their products and services third, they are more likely to engage both their customers and staff emotionally.

When employees are emotionally engaged with a company's purpose that results in higher productivity and performance because individuals want to align their personal and professional goals and values with the company's values and objectives. This is called 'Aligning your personal why with the company why'. When these are aligned you feel more engaged, loyal and committed to your role, team, manager and the company as a whole.

Supporting Sinek's theory, was a research firm Blessingwhite study[4] of 2500 individuals over a 90-day period, the effect of aligning personal goals to organisational objectives had spectacular results:

- Employee engagement went up from 40% to 80%
- Job fit went up from 30% to 60%
- Commitment to career goals went from 20% to 65%
- Retention Risk went down from 85% to 20%

This study shows what mindfulness and the spiritual movement has been trying to say for eons: that when we listen to our own inner truth and follow our inner voice, we are ultimately happier, healthier and wealthier as a result. I think there is a sense in us that recognises a deep truth when we hear it, read it, or see it. I was brought up in a Pentecostal Christian faith and as an adult have had a keen interest in metaphysics, mindfulness, Buddhism, yoga, consciousness and all things 'Law of Attraction'. What pleases me is the links between all of these theologies, and the increasing acceptance of its benefits due to the acceptance of a search for personal truth inside the corporate world.

THE SOCIAL RESPONSIBILITY MOVEMENT

It still pleasantly surprises me when career coaching clients first start to wonder how they can truly be of service and step into their purpose, or how entire organisations strategise how they can be of benefit to their communities or a cause and make a profit. Something I would once have thought would be reserved for not-for profits or the pews of a Christian Church service has been awakened in people everywhere. More people are asking, "What path is right for me?" and "How can I be most fulfilled?" and "How can I best serve others?" than "How can I be the most successful?"

We are growing up with the same messages and conditioning about 'success' as our parents did, but there is a definite shift from 'more is more' to 'real is better' and 'find your truth'. People like Oprah Winfrey and Richard Branson have led the way in helping others see that speaking about intuition and putting people first in corporate organisations is the way to success and fulfilment.

---

4. *Blessingwhite research 2010 quoted in the book Engagement Equation by Blessingwhite consultants; Christopher Rice, Fraser Marlow and Mary Ann Masarech*

Many of us in today's X and Y Generations had parents who may have 'had it all' but are still wondering "Is this all there is?" We are the children of the 'I'm worth it!' generation, and while that is a good thing I think the overall shift to "How can I serve?" feels more true than, "What's in it for me?"

ECONOMIC FACTORS AFFECTING YOUR CAREER

UNEMPLOYMENT

Unemployment is still rising in Australia and an increasing number of jobs are becoming part time. The biggest issue in the labour market however is not that jobs have been declining, but that the only increase in employment has been in part-time jobs. In any case, this book is focusing on unhappy employment or employment that is not aligned with your own truth! At the same time, the rise of unemployment does mean that developing your personal brand is more important than it has ever been.

SISTERS DOING IT FOR THEMSELVES

Women are becoming more entrepreneurial. Australian women are starting small businesses at a higher rate than men and make up one third of all small businesses in the major cities in Australia according to ABS data over the last five years. In the US, women own 36% of all businesses.

According to Forbes Magazine[5], women entrepreneurs are more adept than their male counterparts at seeing gaps in the market and seizing the opportunity, according to The Kauffman Index: Startup Activity. "WBEs [women business enterprises] are agile, innovative problem-solvers, meeting corporations' needs quickly, adapting to marketplace changes and providing deep value and cost-effectiveness," said Pamela Prince Eason, president and CEO of Women's Business Enterprise National Council (WBENC).

This is something I have certainly experienced with almost 70% of my clientele being female. Most of them would like to start a business or do start a business as a result of working with me.

---

5. 8127.0 - *Australian Small Business Operators - Findings from the 2005 and 2006 Characteristics of Small Business Surveys, 2005-06*

Interestingly these businesses are not just self-serving but almost always seek to make their communities or the world a better place.

OUTSOURCING

If the robots won't disrupt your career then globalisation (newly known as near-shoring or outsourcing) will still give it a nudge. Organisations will continue to cycle between in-sourcing and out-sourcing staff and the ease of a mobilised workforce, the cost of full time employees, and a trend toward highly skilled contract workforces through technology portals are the new future.

According to Deloitte's research study on global insourcing and outsourcing these are the trends:

	IT	HR	ACCOUNTING & FINANCE
CURRENTLY OUTSOURCING	75%	30%	37%
PREDICTED FUTURE OUTSOURCING	81%	40%	53%

SO, WHAT DOES THIS MEAN FOR YOU?

As more people are being pushed into part-time work and have less chance to depend on a single organisation to look after their future, it's time to stop waiting for permission and approval. You need to take the control of your career into your own hands so that you can free up your future!

THE EXCITING POSSIBILITIES

The changing face of employment and the world means that you need to discover what you want (by getting in touch with your inner guidance system) and design a path that will help you achieve it. This will help you gain the momentum and meaning you need to truly stand out and perform with excellence.

Every change in society brings challenges, but it also brings great benefits. It's up to you to decide whether these changes will have a positive or negative effect on your career and outlook. As mentioned earlier, The Industrial Revolution put a lot of craftsmen out of work, but it also meant that many people had access to affordable clothing and other products than ever before. The Technological Revolution made typists, shorthand specialists and other technicians redundant, but it opened up a wide world of other opportunities at the same time.

It has never been easier or more acceptable to shape your own career by making the connections, learning the skills, and negotiating the environment and terms you choose. For this reason, this is the perfect time to take a step back from your current work and ask some hard questions. Of course, you don't have to do this at all. You can be like most of your colleagues and simply ignore your uneasiness, dissatisfaction, and lack of enthusiasm for your work and show up each day and 'go through the motions'... at least until you are replaced by a robot, made redundant because your manager finally realises you aren't really engaged, or until some calamity strikes, and you are forced to make changes.

I believe that the Gallup Institute and other studies overstate the role of leadership and management in workforce disengagement, I also believe that effective self-management and self-leadership are key to fulfilment so you can be your best self and do your best work. These skills will be recognised and encouraged more in the workplace, and incorporated into future corporate training programs. An awareness of the processes and diagnostic tools in this book can help you feel in full alignment with your work, and make leaders more effective at selecting and developing staff who are 100% engaged and performing at the top of their game. Just imagine what feeling 100% engaged would do for your own career success or – if you are a leader - your team's productivity and performance!

A NEW APPROACH

The old approach to career choice involved taking some tests at school to determine what you would be good at, studying hard so that you could get into (and successfully complete) the required course, then applying for jobs and steadily moving up the ladder of income and opportunity (assuming you have the connections and skills to do so). Your trajectory was largely determined by your teachers, parents, and mentors, and your career path was fairly well established by your mid-twenties. A certain amount of boredom and endurance was part of the package.

The new approach is quite different. It's much more vibrant, flexible, and positive. Most people don't realise just how much their choices are determined by other people, so they end up in a career which they hate, or which is dissatisfying, working insane hours to buy homes and cars they have no time to enjoy. Your career isn't just about what you do, it's also about what you care about, what you earn, what you like and the lifestyle you choose. What's right for me, is probably not right for you, but if I was an important influence on your career decision, you'd be stuck in a career that met my criteria of success, not yours.

The reality is that technology, the mindfulness movement, and changes in our workplace means that you have the power to shape your career and your life. You don't have to check out of society and live on a subsistence farm in the middle of nowhere to break free of the chains of meaningless work, you can stay in the world, and shape your world and career in whatever way you want.

CHAPTER 3
TOP 10 CAREER MISTAKES

> *"The biggest mistake that you can make is to believe that you are working for somebody else. Job security is gone. The driving force of a career must come from the individual. Remember: Jobs are owned by the company, you own your career!"*
>
> *- Earl Nightingale*

When I first started my blog I was driven to do it because I read one statistic which blew me away. I learned that 80% of people were unhappy in their jobs. Forget about 5% unemployment! What about the majority of our population who hate what they are doing? I just couldn't get this statistic out of my head.

As I did more research into why people were unhappy at work, I wanted to balance that with the success stories of the 20% - the ones who loved what they did. I wanted to understand what these successful people were doing that was different. My goal was to discover how they thought, what decisions they made, and the principles they followed that differed from the unhappy ones.

What I found was pretty simple. The people who were unhappy were largely focused on money and status, and heavily influenced by other people. This book focuses on the things that make people love their job, but before we dive into that I'd like to briefly discuss the ten biggest mistakes people make when it comes to managing their career.

These ten mistakes really do hold you back from having the career of your dreams:

1. **BEING REACTIVE:** There are two types of job seeking activity: reactive and proactive. Most people are reactive. They jump onto online job boards, see what is available and apply for roles. Others wait to be noticed or to hear of job opportunities within their own organisation. They are simply responding to demand that is pushed out by others. Reactive job seeking does not take into account any longer term plans or alignment with personal goals and values.

I was speaking to a coaching client once who worked for a medium-sized online organisation. He was surprised that after five years at the organisation no-one had put him on a leadership development program. I asked him if he had spoken to anyone about being put on the plan and he said, "No, I am waiting to be asked!"

2. **NOT HAVING CLEAR GOALS:** Dr. Gail Matthews, a psychology professor at Dominican University in California, did a study on goal-setting with 267 participants. She found that you are 42% more likely to achieve your goals just by writing them down.[6]

Most people don't plan their career in advance. So, if they are made redundant they panic and take the first job they are offered as they have no backup plan. Since they have no long term plan they have no idea whether a particular opportunity fits in with their true path and they are always unsure about what to do. They rely on others' opinions before making their career decisions. These people are cruising through life, living for the weekends with no thought of the longer-term picture and taking no responsibility for personal professional development.

3. **LACK OF SELF-AWARENESS:** Some people are not aware of their passions, values, and dreams. They don't take these things into account when making career decisions, nor are they aware of their strengths and weaknesses.

Jade Yap from the famous blog "The Tiny Buddha" writes about her own career planning mistakes and how she was able to find herself, "The only thing that really helped me was taking time out to really understand and learn about myself. Through my struggles, I identified that I was always working toward goals I thought other people wanted for me."

---

6. Dr Gail Matthews research study on goal setting http://www.dominican.edu/dominicannews/dominican-research-cited-in-forbes-article

After some introspection she completely changed the direction of her career. She also advises us to, "...take the time to try things and see what you enjoy, don't worry about 'fitting in', don't try to justify your worth with money and things and let go of expectations." Realise that your life is not set in stone and you are in the driving seat. Once Jade was able to do this, she was able to plan and create a career that was perfect for her.

4. **BEING OVERLY INFLUENCED BY OTHERS:** Citi, in partnership with LinkedIn, released their 'fifth wave of research' on the career and financial issues affecting professionals.[7] One topic they explored in this 'wave' was who influenced the career path that professionals take. What they found was that even well into their 30s and 40s professionals have been shaped by their childhood career dreams and are still influenced by their mothers, fathers or early mentors - like the career guidance counsellor from high school.

This doesn't seem like a major problem, but when you seek the advice of others rather than yourself in your career decisions you may be looking for approval from others, rather than thinking about what truly engages and fulfils you.

When we leave school and university we have little confidence in ourselves. We often overlook our innermost desires and go with what our parents, or school career counsellor tells us will be an ideal fit for our careers. Sometimes we are even influenced by the need to keep up with the Jones' and take on entire career plans in order to please a childhood influence. The best person to guide your life should always be you.

5. **BEING FOCUSED ON MONEY:** After university comes a decade that can include large study loan repayments, weddings, children, and mortgages. You may be forgiven for thinking it's smart to take the job that pays the greatest amount of money. The problem with this thinking is that ten years down the track you will have commitments you can't get out of, a job you hate, and a life full of stress and anxiety. This is not a price you want to pay.

In a recent CIO Magazine article about career regret, the author interviewed 30 people across many different industries and levels in their career. One story stood out in particular: a CEO of a large company who said that he hated going to work every single day but his large salary had led him to lead an expensive life.

---

7. *Citi and Linked In Research Paper - Firth Wave of Research* http://www.businesswire.com/multimedia/home/20141028005207/en/

He wished he could quit and do something he enjoyed but he just couldn't afford to do it. Talk about golden handcuffs!

6. **LACK OF SELF BELIEF:** Some people choose to think they are not strong enough to believe they can create a career they love.

In Christina Guidotti's book, *True Believers* she says that a 'True Believer' has the three superpowers of belief, conviction and commitment to reach fulfilment. As Steve Jobs says in his 7 Rules for Success, "Dream bigger. See genius in your craziness, believe in yourself, believe in your vision, and be constantly prepared to defend those ideas."

7. **NOT INVESTING IN YOURSELF:** People who do minimum education, training, reading, experiential learning or personal development to develop themselves and their career prospects aren't doing themselves any favours.

To invest in yourself think about these five things:

- Invest in your strengths and use them more frequently

- Invest in gaining skills and apply them actively

- Invest in the right relationships and give them time and attention

- Invest in a career or business coach and sustain your momentum

- Invest in your family and personal life to create balance and strengthen your career

Ben Siong, the manager of Australian Strength Performance has travelled to the Poliquin Institute in Rhode Island (USA) numerous times. One year, he spent $50K - $60K on his own training and development. This led to huge advantages for him. He is now a Level 4 Poliquin trainer, one of only six in Australia. That niche training and certification has enabled him to position himself and his business as a specialised training institute where he trains trainers and athletes. Without investing in himself he would not be in this position.

8. **NOT MARKETING YOURSELF WELL:** Some people's CV, cover letter, LinkedIn profile and phone follow-ups are not hitting the messaging mark and communicating that they are the perfect candidates for their dream jobs.

One of my clients named John had an impressive career in IT yet was scared to market himself as he didn't know how to do it effectively. The more I spoke to him about his job-hunting behaviours, the more he realised the importance of solid communication documents, social media profiles and the ability to verbalise his 'elevator pitch' on the phone. If you can do these things you are likely to land an interview – and that is the main goal of those documents. Once John polished up his documents and created a laser targeted elevator pitch, he started getting the interviews and job offers that he was looking for.

9. **NOT LEARNING HOW THE JOB HUNTING WORLD REALLY WORKS:** People waste time on the wrong methods of applying for jobs, they do not engage recruiters appropriately, they don't know how to uncover roles in the hidden job market, to create opportunities, or to analyse a job ad or position description properly. In addition, they are hopeless at networking with purpose and they are unable to identify and connect with key decision makers.

Chelsea didn't know how to do any of these things at first. When she learned how to tailor her job hunting activity and focus her networking efforts on the right people she stopped wasting time and was able to communicate her value effectively to new connections. This change in behavior led to three new job opportunities coming to her that she didn't even apply for!

10. **TOTALLY SCREWING UP INTERVIEWS (EVEN WHEN THEY HAVE EVERYTHING THE COMPANY WANTS!):** 99.9% of the 10,000 candidates I have interviewed over the last 12 years didn't know how to answer behavioural questions. Companies are increasingly relying on matching people's behaviour to the job and company as well as their skills. If you are not able to demonstrate that you have that proven behaviour then you will not progress to an offer.

If you're making any of these mistakes then you are seriously jeopardising your potential to land your dream jobs.

WHAT ABOUT THE OTHER SIDE?

Imagine if 99.5% of the job seeking population gets these things wrong. What happens when you do these things well? What happens when you don't just avoid making these mistakes, but you actually have a plan to do things right? You can just click your fingers and multiple opportunities will appear in front of you. You can easily create images of your dream career and turn them into reality by connecting with the people who can make things happen for you.

The best way to take control of your career is to work through the exercises in this book and start the journey of knowing yourself.

PART 2

THE EPIC CAREER QUEST

CHAPTER 4
HEART-MIND CONNECTION

"Heart coherence occurs when the heart and mind work together in a genuine connection."
— Rachel Sparkes

As you set out on your Epic Career Quest, you'll need to do some work on yourself because along the way you are going to face obstacles and road blocks that will tempt you to quit. After all, what hero ever achieved a worthwhile quest without facing some pretty big challenges?

In your journey through this book you will focus on changing what's going on in your mind and heart so that you get lasting results. We will start by working through some activities that will expose your fears, beliefs, values, strengths, and weaknesses. These six steps are probably the most challenging parts of your journey, and this is the stage when people most often call me and ask for a one-to-one consultation. You'll be diving deep inside your own mind and heart, and evaluating things you may have been ignoring or taking for granted for years. Let's look at some of the foundational aspects of this heart-mind connection.

TAKING RESPONSIBILITY

Many times when people come to me for career advice they think the issue is external. They say things like:

- "Oh, I hate my boss, he is making my life a living hell!"
- "My work is unfulfilling."
- "I don't get paid enough."
- "My company is not flexible enough."
- "I don't have enough opportunities to advance."
- "I have to pay too much in fees and taxes to start my own business."

If all of these things were 100% true, then people who get pay rises, move jobs, or get new managers would be totally fine and live happily ever after. But that is not the case. According to the ABS data[8], the average time people spent in a role was only 18 months! People are changing jobs almost as often as they change jeans but they are not finding the peace and fulfillment they are searching for. The truth is that you can only find that peace and fulfillment when you are connected with your true self and working in a career that honors who you are.

To really love your job and start connecting with the greatest version of you in your career, you need to take responsibility for where you are, do the inner work that is required and accept that transformation is 100% about knowing what's important to you and honoring that in all your career decisions. It's about listening to what's going on inside your mind and inside your heart.

HEART COHERENCE

The US research institute HeartMath, calls the heart-mind connection 'heart coherence'. Heart coherence occurs when the heart and mind work together in a genuine connection. Over the past 20 years the institute of HeartMath has produced scientific research which shows that when a person shifts into heart coherence, the heart and brain operate synergistically as a single system so that they maximise energy and prevent stress-producing patterns while increasing our mental

---

8. Labour Mobility 2012 http://www.abs.gov.au/ausstats/abs@.nsfdossbytitle/3AC28A55A52B926ECA256BD00026E69B

clarity, and capacity for discernment. For many people this only happens by chance rather than by deliberate intention.

HeartMath's new research suggests that our energetic, or spiritual, heart is an access point for our natural inner technology. By accessing the heart's intuitive intelligence we can elevate our communications, decisions, and choices to a much higher level of effectiveness. This research into the intuitive, energetic heart bears out what people have associated with their inner voice throughout history. According to HeartMath, the energetic heart communicates a steady stream of intuitive information to the mind and brain, which we often ignore because our ego choices override the intuitive suggestions we hear.

Access to our heart's intuition varies, yet we all have it to some degree. As we learn to slow our mind and tune into our deeper heart feelings, this natural intuitive connection can occur. Intuitive insights are like energetic gold and often lead us into deeper understanding of ourselves and of others.

This means that as you embark on your Epic Career Quest your first task is to slow down, listen to your heart, and practice getting into a state of heart coherence.

DEVELOPING HEART COHERENCE

In order to take advantage of the energetic and stress-reducing benefits of heart coherence you need to pay attention to what's going on in your mind, and listen to your heart. We're not used to doing this and many people would almost rather die than face their fears and their inner selves. However, the good news is that it's your brain and your heart. No-one else can see inside them, and there is no-one to blame but yourself for what is going on in there. Facing your deepest fears and healing them is the first step on the road to creating the career you want. It's all up to you and you can change if you want to.

You've already committed to this journey, remember, because you are sick of the life you're living right now. So, it's probably not surprising that the first step on your journey, developing heart coherence, requires courage and tenacity.

You'll need courage to do things that scare you. Things that make you uncomfortable. Things that take you outside your comfort zone so you can grow.

The path to loving your job doesn't happen in a cosy cocoon. It takes deep soul searching in a radical, powerful way. And that means it's going to take a lot of guts.

You'll need tenacity to keep on going when the journey gets hard. You'll need to try new approaches until you get what you want. That means knocking on new doors, making new contacts, trying new processes, approaching new investors, finding new ingredients to fix anything that is not working. You'll need a 'never say die' attitude when you hit roadblocks on the way to your new career along with the discipline to be kind to yourself and choose to quieten your inner critic and continue on your path despite any self-doubt and anxiety that pops up along the way.

All this is part of the essential foundation you need to put in place before you really start working on your road map. At some stage during coaching there comes a pivotal point where all this just 'clicks' for my clients. I call it the 'shift'. At first you may have no idea what you want, but once you open up to the ideas of intuition and values-based goals and get in a mindset where 'anything is possible' you tune into your heart coherence and suddenly 'the shift' happens.

This happens to every single client I work with, no matter how driven they are or how lost they are. They all have an idea of what their 'truth' is (what their inner voice is saying to them). For some it's so confronting and scary that they like to drown it out or become angry and aggressive, and for others it's like a wall falling down and I can see the tears welling up as suddenly they have permission to be who they were always meant to be in this life. It's such a gift for me to be able to sit across from someone and say, "I see you." For some people, the first time they say it out loud for others is like returning home.

CASE STUDY
HEARTS AND MIND: THANKYOU WATER

Thank You Water call themselves a 'Consumer Movement'. They empower you to fund life-changing projects through simple choices in your everyday life. In 2008, Daniel Flynn and Justine Flynn were at university. They were working on their five year plans and learned about the world water crisis and the fact that 900 million people didn't have access to clean drinking water. They also learned that Australians spend $600 million per year on bottled water! So, they decided to start a social enterprise, take some market share of the bottled water industry in Australia and send the profits to countries like Africa where they really need access to fresh, clean water.

The company has since branched out into personal care products and food that also contribute to providing water, food, or health and hygiene training to people in need. Every cent of the profits go to these life changing projects and you can even track the exact details of the project complete with village information and GPS coordinates by using their 'track your impact' page system.

This company is mind blowing! It has all the elements of a purpose driven business. When Justine and Daniel started out they were just university students. So you could say that their idea was more of a calling or a mission to begin with. They loved the idea, but hadn't figured out how to make it profitable yet. Eventually, they proved they were good at what they were doing, and they made it profitable so they were able to redistribute the money to the cause they cared about.

CHAPTER 5
PASSION AND PURPOSE

"Oh the Power and the Passion!"
- Midnight Oil

There are many different opinions concerning the role of passion and purpose in crafting a career plan that you love. In my experience it is important to be very clear about what passion and purpose mean to you personally, and how they influence your overall direction. The word 'passion' comes from a Greek word meaning 'to suffer'. This represents a very strong feeling about some person or thing. Modern definitions of passion range from, "a friendly or eager interest in or admiration for a cause, discovery, or activity", to "a feeling of unusual excitement, enthusiasm or compelling emotion, a positive affinity or love, towards a subject."

Within the context of your career, I define passion as the things you do, or ideas you have, that you really like or even love. Those things that make time pass rapidly, energise you and come so naturally you feel like you were born to do them.

PASSION IS THE CURIOSITY IN YOUR CAREER

I once went to hear Oprah Winfrey speak live in Melbourne. I wrote notes for the entire two-hour talk and was completely mesmerised by her spiritual wisdom. Much of what she had to say concerned tapping into your intuition (or heart coherence) when making life decisions, including those related to your career. Oprah says that your purpose or calling is based on whatever you are curious about, so you should listen to your curiosity and honour it. Many people get confused because they think purpose needs to be something big and grand. But it doesn't really. Purpose is the thing you do, or the role you play, that makes people feel a certain way about you.

Curiosity is generally the North Star that guides you to your passions if you are not sure what they are. These are the things you are interested in, including the subjects and ideas you like to read about, talk about, and research. The courses you attend, Facebook posts you read, magazine subscriptions you pay for and the user groups you are part of all indicate your areas of curiosity.

I am fascinated by extra-terrestrial life and anything to do with telecommunications, electricity and energy. I'm not sure where I picked up these interests but my recent nights on the internet have included watching documentaries on the Serbian-American inventor Nikola Tesla. Tesla invented the alternating current electric motor as well as wireless communication. Many believe he was also screwed over by Thomas Edison in the race to win the electricity war.

Underlying this curiosity is my fascination with how things connect and influence each other, and the potential for the unknown. I am deeply passionate about these things and these interests permeate my conversations with others, the programs I create for clients, and every aspect of my business. Exploring these curiosities of mine helped me to find my passions and purpose, which is to help other people achieve their career potential and make the connections they need to become influencers.

IDENTIFYING YOUR PASSIONS

Some of you probably know exactly what you are passionate about and have a list of things in your head already. If you aren't clear about your passions, here are some great questions to ask yourself when trying to figure out what you actually like doing:-

- What sort of activities lift your spirits and feed your energy?

Passion and Purpose

- What activities make time disappear for you?
- What activities are 'pure fun' for you?
- Are there things that you've always loved to do but not focused on fully?
- When do you feel that you are being most true to your own self?
- What are things you do that give you a burning/excited feeling in your stomach?
- What are you curious about?
- What lights you up?
- What do you invest your time and energy into?

Think about these questions and write your answers down. They will lead you down the path of your passions if you don't already know what they are. You'll also want to put pictures of these things on your vision board so you can keep them front and centre as you think about your ideal career and pursue your Epic Career Quest because they will keep you focused and motivated.

PURPOSE IS THE MEANING IN YOUR CAREER.

> *"If passion is the driver of your career, the thing that helps you get up early and stay up late working, then purpose is the meaning of your career, the thing that enables you to do and bear almost anything in order to succeed."*
> *- Rachel Sparkes*

Viktor Frankl, an Austrian existential psychologist and concentration camp survivor, created a school of thought called logotherapy. Frankl surmised that our dominant driving force is to find meaning in life. His book, *Man's Search for Meaning*, explores his observation of what drove both prisoners and guards to cling to life and values, or to descend into despair. Nietzsche nicely sums up his philosophy on how people were able to survive the camps: "He who has a 'why' to live for can bear almost any 'how'."

Frankl went on to say that you have to focus on a cause greater than your own personal gain in order to apply real meaning and purpose to your life and career. You might say he focused on the 'indirect approach' to getting what you want from life, that is the approach of giving and serving, rather than demanding and getting. So, if you want people to love you: then start by loving people and serving them! If you want more money; then help people make money. If you want more joy in life; then give joy to other people. In fact, I suggest that the more we give, the more we'll love our career and our lives in general.

Finally, I'd like to quote Frankl's view of how to succeed, "Don't aim at success. The more you aim at it and make it a target, the more you are going to miss it. For success, like happiness, cannot be pursued; it must ensue, and it only does so as the unintended side effect of one's personal dedication to a cause greater than oneself or as the by-product of one's surrender to a person other than oneself."

THE KEY TO THE PURPOSE PUZZLE

Maslow's Hierarchy of Basic Needs identifies both a micro level of purpose and a macro level of purpose. Jacob Sokol, author of *Living on Purpose – An Uncommon Guide to Finding, Living, and Rocking Your Life's Purpose*, defines your micro level purpose as knowing your values and living in integrity with them. As he says, when you know what you stand for, and do what you believe in, your confidence and sense of self-worth will be sky-high, regardless of how much your situation sucks. This takes Maslow's suggestion that you work to fulfil your physiological and safety needs by earning money, to another level.

But that is only half of the picture. On a macro level your purpose is sharing in service to others, it is about giving, not getting. We all want to reach the Self-Actualised needs stage of Maslow's Hierarchy. We want to better ourselves and improve our lives, but purpose--like success and happiness--is counterintuitive, so if we truly want to make our own lives better, we need to make a positive contribution to the rest of the world, whether that involves one other person, a community, a nation, or the planet.

Throughout the 20th Century psychology and neuroscience have been obsessed with discovering why we do what we do. Sigmund Freud said that our behaviour is motivated purely by sex and aggression, that everything we do is designed to gain pleasure and avoid pain. On a primal level, this ties in with Paul MacLean's Triune Brain Model which says you have three parts to your brain:

1. The reptilian (instinctual) part which handles things like territory and aggression.
2. The mammalian (emotional) part which handles belonging, food, and sex.
3. The primate (thinking) part which focuses on things like perception, planning, and handling complex concepts. This is the part of your brain that knows deep down that you need meaning in your life, and it's the part that Freud ignored. This part of your brain is the part that drives your Epic Career Quest.

IDENTIFYING YOUR PURPOSE

Here are some questions that will help you uncover your purpose. Answer them honestly and in writing if possible.

- Why are you doing what you do in your career?
- What is the purpose of you getting up in the morning, getting dressed, catching the tram or driving your car into work, then doing what you do all day?
- Are you doing all that just to put a roof over your head and food on the table?
- Is your need to belong and receive love being met through friends at work?
- Do you receive recognition and gain a sense of accomplishment in your career?
- Are you achieving your full potential, including your need for creative expression and being all you can be at work?
- Is satisfaction, recognition, and excellence the full expression of your purpose?

CASE STUDY

PASSION AND PURPOSE: 'WHO GIVES A CRAP' TOILET PAPER

I just love this company! Firstly, because they are hilariously funny and totally real when it comes to toilet humour. When you order their products personality literally oozes from the paper. Secondly, because their purpose is to make the world a better place!

Who Gives A Crap was started by three mates, Simon, Jehan, and Danny, in 2012. They learnt that 2.5 billion people across the world don't have access to a toilet. That's roughly 40% of the global population and means that diarrhoea-related diseases fill over half of sub-Saharan African hospital beds and kill 1,400 children under five every day. They thought that was pretty crap. So, in July 2012, they launched Who Gives A Crap with a crowdfunding campaign on IndieGoGo. Apparently Simon sat on a toilet in their draughty warehouse and refused to move until they had raised enough pre-orders to start production. According to their website it took 50 hours and one cold bottom, but they raised over $50,000 to get their company off the ground! They delivered the first product in March 2013 and have been growing ever since.

Speaking from personal experience their whole customer experience is amazing. I use their toilet paper, tissues, and paper towels. They are made from bamboo, so no trees are used at all in the making of the toilet paper and 50% of their profits go to WaterAid to build toilets and improve sanitation in the developing world. They deliver to your door and you can even arrange a subscription so you will never run out of loo paper again. It won't even cost you more than the other mass produced, tree burning, environment-destroying, profit mongering brands. Their tissues have lovely feel good messages on the boxes and there are great tips and ideas on what you can do with the wrapping paper to recycle.

Their mission statement is: "We always want to stay true to our roots: toilet humour and making the world a better place." This is a great example of a group of people who started with the goal of making the world a better place, then figured out how to get good at what they did, make it profitable, and worked out they loved it

CHAPTER 6
THE DECISION DIAL

"You are never a prisoner to your past as long as you choose to change."

- Sigmund Freud

Your journey to personal awakening and reaching your highest career potential will not always be an easy one. Sometimes everything will move smoothly forwards, then suddenly you will hit a roadblock, lose motivation, and feel stuck. I think that one of the most common complaints I have heard from my clients during my 15+ years as an HR Consultant, recruiter, and coach is; "I feel stuck, and I don't know why or what to do about it."

Because some of the issues you will face in your personal awakening can be confronting, the Decision Dial is a tool I developed to help my clients get past that roadblock and move forwards. Whenever you are stuck, you can use this to help you decide whether you are willing to pay the price of progress or not. It's OK to choose to ignore some things, you can always come back to them later. Moving forward, the good news is that all you need to do is make three decisions: two small decisions, and one big decision!

Imagine you are looking at a safe with a dial lock as you can see in the illustration over the page.

The dial is divided into four parts and each part represents a decision. As you choose to move forward with each decision the dial moves to the right, finally landing on the fourth part and unlocking the safe which contains the key to your career potential. If you decide to ignore the decision and stick with your existing situation, that's OK. You may not be ready to move forward yet.

THE DECISION DIAL

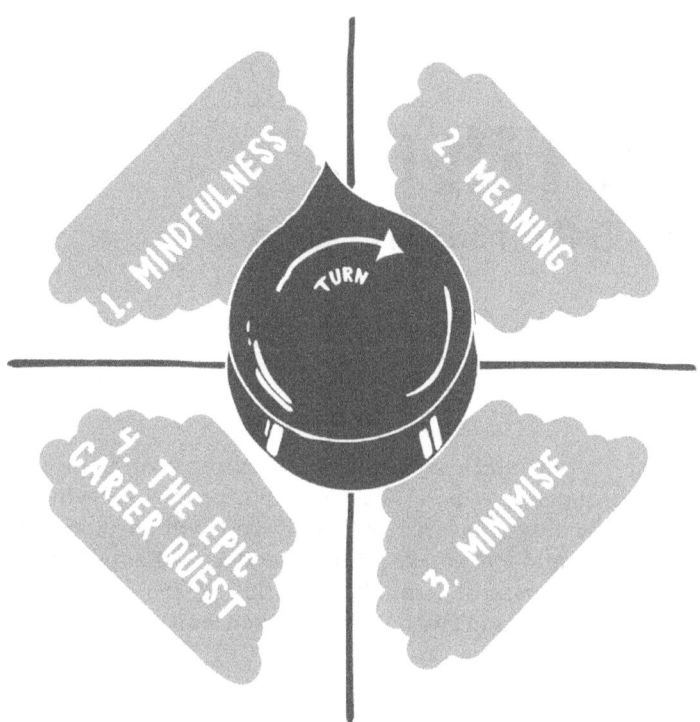

Every decision begins at *Dial Position #1:* **MINDFULNESS**.

Here, you are just becoming aware that something needs to change in your career. Generally, one of three things has happened to cause this awareness:

1. **WAKE UP CALL:** A tragedy or shocking incident has happened and jolted you into new awareness. Maybe you have been made redundant or got fired out of the blue.

2. **CAREER BREAK:** You have taken a break and started to review your situation e.g. maternity leave, redundancy or career sabbatical.

3. **GROWING ANXIETY:** You are aware of a small voice inside telling you something is not right. You can't put your finger on it, but it seems to grow louder each day.

At this point, you have a small decision to make: Small Decision #1. You can either:

a) Ignore it; or

b) Choose more meaning in your career.

If you ignore it, nothing changes. If you choose more meaning in your career the dial clicks one position to the right. You are now at

Dial Position #2: **MEANING.**

Here you have decided to pursue a career with more personal meaning. In this instance 'meaning' is the pursuit of work that has the following attributes:

1. **PURPOSE** – You consider your personal 'why'.

2. **LEGACY** – You consider how you want to be remembered and what you want to leave behind.

3. **CONTRIBUTION** – You consider what contribution your work makes to other people, to society and even to the planet.

4. **FULFILMENT** – You desire joy and satisfaction through your work.

Now you need to make another small decision. Will you:

a) Ignore it; or

b) Choose to minimise to enable mobility.

Once again, if you decide to ignore it, nothing changes. But, if you choose more meaning in your career the dial clicks one more position to the right and you are at *Dial Position #3:* **MINIMISE.**

Here you come face-to-face with the things you need to minimise, overcome, or let go of in order to progress. These 'things' may not be physical things. They could be ideas, memories or values. Often the things you need to minimise are so ingrained in you that it may seem as though you need to cut off a part of yourself. This is one of the hardest places to be and people who feel 'stuck' are often at this point for many years only to find that when they finally decide they have had enough and let go or minimise, change and progress happen at incredible speed. The truth is, as Sigmund Freud said, "You are never a prisoner to your past as long as you choose to change."

Things to minimise include the following:

1. **YOUR EGO:** This is the hardest thing to minimise. Your ego keeps you holding on to things and titles outside yourself that give you a sense of worth. When you start to minimise your need for external validation, you also shed the need to hold onto things that may be holding you back from making new career decisions.

2. **YOUR FEARS:** Facing and minimising your fear of potential failure or success will get you unstuck and moving forward. The trick is to identify what you are actually afraid of. Often it is helpful to have someone who cares about your outcome, but who is not part of the problem to work through this with you. Fears are tricky things, which is why they are so powerful.

3. **YOUR BELIEFS:** If you've ever found yourself thinking things like, "I'm just not good enough" or "It's not possible for me", or "I can't do that," you know exactly what I mean. Identifying your limiting beliefs and minimising them through action will give you enormous momentum.

4. **YOUR INFLUENCES:** Most of us are totally unaware how much power we allow external influences to have over us. Some people stay in particular careers until retirement just to impress their parents! You need to identify your past and current influences so that you can make new decisions based on what's right for you.

Now, you come to **THE BIG DECISION!** Once again, you can:

a) Ignore it; or

b) Choose absolute commitment to change.

This is not an easy decision because once you make this decision there is no going back! That is why it's called **THE BIG DECISION**. If you choose absolute commitment to change you will need to work hard, you will need to learn, to evolve, and to change. You will probably need to confront parts of yourself you've been hiding from for years. It won't be easy, but you can bet your bottom dollar it will be worth it.

Most people will stop here, play it safe, and choose to ignore their discomfort and their nagging desire for more. A few will take the 'road less travelled'. Which one will you choose?

If you choose absolute commitment to change, the dial clicks one more position to the right. Shazaaaam! You hear the magical sound of the safe unlocking!

Congratulations! You are now at *Dial Position #4:* You have chosen **THE EPIC CAREER QUEST!**

The door creaks open to show you the incredible vision of your career potential. Since you have decided that you will pursue a career that is in alignment with your true self no matter what, you are no longer satisfied with your current path. With this decision made, you will discover the right path for you to travel, and you will make it happen.

You now have a deep personal reason why you want this new career and it is extremely important to you. You have decided that you will go on a journey to get it, even though you don't know exactly where your quest will lead, or exactly what it is you want to do. So you are absolutely committed to finding it and you know that you won't stop until you have found and are doing the work you love.

Welcome! Your journey has begun.

BARRIERS TO DECISION MAKING

Before we leave this section, I'd like to make a few comments. It may seem obvious that moving forward toward your own Epic Career Quest is a really good idea. But many people get stuck somewhere on this decision dial, others move through it, but are thrown backwards by the responses of well-meaning friends and relatives. You may recognise some of your own reasons for not moving forward in the list below. Simply identifying them and asking yourself if you want these things to define you may set you free.

1. FEAR OF SUCCESS

As Marianne Williamson so beautifully put it, sometimes we are not afraid of our inadequacies, sometimes we are afraid of our power!

"Our deepest fear is not that we are inadequate. Our deepest fear is that we are powerful beyond measure. It is our light, not our darkness that most frightens us. We ask ourselves, "Who am I to be brilliant, gorgeous, talented, fabulous?" Actually, who are you not to be? You are a child of God. Your playing small does not serve the world. There is nothing enlightened about shrinking so that other people won't feel insecure around you. We are all meant to shine, as children do. We were born to make manifest the glory of God that is within us. It's not just in some of us; it's in everyone. And as we let our own light shine, we unconsciously give other people permission to do the same. As we are liberated from our own fear, our presence automatically liberates others."

What would happen if you committed to the best career ever? Well, you would have to stop whining about the fact that you don't have one for a start. This can be hard for some people as they are so good at playing victim roles that the thought of changing to a hero role is reason enough to do nothing.

2. CONFUSION

The thought of not loving your job for the rest of your life plagues your mind every second of every day. You seek the help of coaches, friends, and psychologists yet your head continues to spin and you just can't get out of the career hell that you feel trapped in.

You need to develop self-awareness and work through a step-by-step process to gain clarity about who you really are, where you want to go, and how to get there. It needs to be an ordered and powerful process so you can get out of your head, into your heart, and then act through your hands.

3. CONCERN

You are afraid of not knowing or finding your passion or purpose. You avoid going out with friends or attending dinner parties because you are not proud of what you do. You dread people asking because it feels like you are being fake or you are so over your career you can't stand to talk about it at all. You have zero passion and zero interest in talking about your job and so your social life is suffering.

The answer is do something! You don't have to know your passion or purpose right away. You just have to follow your curiosity and take small actions toward those things. The only antidote to fear is action.

4. FEAR OF LOSING MONEY OR STATUS

You don't love your job, it's hard to feel passionate about it and you have become disengaged. But you get paid a stack of cash to do it. You're used to a particular lifestyle and it's very hard to drop it all to do what you really want to do, right?

Hell no! When you are not in flow, and you feel disengaged, opportunities to learn pass you by along with opportunities for promotion and financial advancement. Little by little you become less engaged in your current career. This means your potential for earning will also dry up over time.

You need to take action immediately and get back into your sweet spot, so that you don't dread work. It may not be as hard as you think, sometimes a little tweak here and there does the trick.

A WORD ON 'MINIMALISM'

About a year ago I went to a free talk by 'The Minimalists'. These two American guys had the American dream: High paying jobs in the IT industry, big cars, and big houses. But they didn't have freedom, happiness, or fulfilment. One of them came across the *minimalist* movement which essentially challenges you to strip yourself of many of your material possessions and material-based desires in order to have more freedom, and to increase your happiness and fulfilment.

They did their research and found that there were varying degrees of minimalism. Some people sold all their worldly possessions and took off to see the world with everything they had left in a back pack. Others just downsized certain parts of their lives, like unpacking a drawer or cupboard each week to see what you actually use. It wasn't a set of rules, it was just an experiment with a range of options to explore what made your life easier, less cluttered, and more energised.

One experiment they did really struck me. They decided to pack up their entire house into boxes and only take out things as they actually 'needed' them for an entire month. So, toothbrushes, plates, and things for guests did get taken out of the boxes but everything else stayed in the boxes. At the end of the month anything left inside the boxes was sold, donated, or ditched!

Everything? Yes, everything! This experiment showed one participant that about 80% of his stuff was not used or even thought of during that month. He realised that he had a huge house just to store stuff he didn't need. He was paying an expensive mortgage for an overpriced storage unit. As a result, he downsized from a five-bedroom house with a double garage to a small, inner city apartment with no car space, since he also decided to sell his car and ride or walk everywhere.

The minimalism movement made him realise that his stuff and his house owned him, not the other way around. Once he became aware of the fact that he was holding onto stuff that he didn't truly value, he was able to let go of it and have much more freedom in his life. By minimising his stuff and his lifestyle he could also eventually afford to quit his job and start building a career he wanted.

If you are feeling the pinch, or feeling trapped by your job, I suggest you take a look at your stuff. Does it own you or do you own it? Even if you own it, how much are you really paying to store it? Minimise so you can mobilise and see what happens in your career, in your relationship, in your finances and in your life. I suspect you might just find more freedom, happiness and fulfilment along the way.

THE REAL COSTS OF AN UNHAPPY CAREER

Loving your career is more than a fleeting feeling or feel-good self-indulgence. It's crucial to the survival of your body, mind, and spirit. It's also crucial to your unique contribution to the world, and to your relationships. I want you to really think about the costs of you not embarking on the career you love.

- **PHYSICAL COSTS:** Do you turn to overeating, drugs, or alcohol to escape the awful feeling of spending most of your waking life making money doing something you don't love? A friend I know is now on anti-depressants and sleeping pills because of his anxiety from working in a job he hates.

- **EMOTIONAL COSTS:** Do you wake up in the morning and feel a pit of dread and anxiety in your stomach? You feel nothing but annoyance at the tasks you do at work and at the end of a long day you are exhausted from doing things that don't fulfil you or inspire you. You get angry at your colleagues or your family and you may feel depressed because you are not being true to yourself.

- **SPIRITUAL COSTS:** Do you feel like your soul is dying because you deny that special magic, that special gift that only you have to give to the world? With each day that passes that voice inside you gets quieter and you feel like your soul is slowly being crushed by a job you don't love.

- **RELATIONSHIP COSTS:** Do you come home unhappy after a day's work and your whole household feels it? Maybe you're miserable so you fight with your partner and tell your kids to go away. Is there no joy in your home? Does everyone walk on eggshells around you, just because you are not fulfilled in your job?

These are real costs that people tell me about every day. I know the price you pay to stay in a job you don't love because I experienced them myself and I know that my life (and that of hundreds of clients) was transformed when I finally acknowledged that the price I was paying was too high.

WHAT ARE THE POSITIVE SIDE EFFECTS OF LOVING YOUR JOB?

- **MENTALLY:** You are on an upward spiral. You wake up with a spring in your step excited to see what each day brings. You are able to visualise and plan your future and feel the blessings of that life you visualised opening before you. You start believing that anything is possible and your goals and dreams get bigger and better. New doors and possibilities open to you because you have made a mental shift that is attracting opportunities into your life like never before. You are free of worry, free of fear and totally grateful that you are able to do what you love every day and truly say, "I Heart My Job".

- **SOCIALLY:** Amazing people who are doing amazing things with their careers will gravitate towards you. You will bounce off each other's energy and opportunities will open up that you would never have imagined before. Your friends and family will pour love and joy back into you as you are able to tap into an infinite source of divine love and joy and share it with the people in your life.

- **FINANCIALLY:** You will make more money than you ever thought possible. You will lose all fear and anxiety about your future because you will feel secure in the value of the special gift that you are sharing with the world and know you are being paid for it. Wayne Dyer says, 'Doing what you love is the cornerstone of having abundance in your life.'

- **SPIRITUALLY:** You are now in daily conversation with your inner spirit and aware of its power, wisdom, and guiding force. You listen and learn from yourself and know that everything you will ever need can be found within. Because you trust yourself and love yourself, when you look in the mirror each day you know you are making a living by being true to yourself and your soul expands with joy. Your spirit shines through everything you do in your career and in every area of your life.

- **EMOTIONALLY:** You are truly happy, and even when roadblocks and challenges come your way you smash through them with tenacity and guts. You know what you want, you are clear in your purpose and you stay calm and focused while going about your business. You feel excited about each day, week and year ahead and you feel confident that you can face whatever the future holds. Most of all you are overflowing with gratitude for the life you have created and the love and abundance that is just around the corner.

- **PHYSICALLY:** You love your job and want to keep in peak physical condition. You now have an abundance of energy so you can attend your gym classes or go for a run and you know exactly what your body needs to keep healthy and fit. You nourish your body with healthy food and give it great exercise and rest because you just can't wait to get up tomorrow and do the work you love with maximum energy and focus.

- **RELATIONSHIPS:** You pour time, effort, love, respect, gratitude and fun into your relationship. If you don't currently have an intimate relationship you are in the perfect position to attract your perfect mate. You are fulfilled as a person and able to be kind and understanding for your partner because you no longer feel trapped in your career. You are joyful, passionate, excited and enthusiastic about your life and full of contagious energy. You can't wait to share your day with your partner and play with your kids. Your home is filled with laughter and joy and you talk about each other's passions and dreams and encourage each other to pursue them. Your family trusts you, and you are in a position to guide them toward a career that they love so they, too, can say, "I Heart My Job" when they grow up. As Marc Anthony says "If you do what you love, you'll never work a day in your life'

PART 3:

THE CAREER COMPASS

CHAPTER 7
THE CAREER NAVIGATORS ROADMAP

"Seek the path that demands your whole being."
- Rumi

A PATH APPEARS

One of the first things that my clients ask for help with is sorting out the clutter in their minds. Many people want to be more fulfilled and happy. They recognise something needs to change but they are at a total loss when it comes to answering the question, "So, where do you actually want your career to take you?"

I absolutely understand this dilemma! My own journey to clarity took me nearly two years on a yoga mat, and involved a lot of heartbreak and struggle, but it doesn't have to take that long, and helping you move from confusion to clarity faster is one of the goals of this book.

The key to gaining clarity is self-awareness. It's fostering that heart coherence and understanding your individual purpose and passion that we spoke about in the first part of this book.

In addition to meditation and other activities that tap into your intuition, there are other practical steps you can take to understand all parts of yourself better, so that you can make clear, authentic decisions about your future career.

The way I do this with my clients is to introduce them to The Career Compass as seen in the image below. This helps them identify where they are currently at on their career lifecycle and also leads to a Career Navigators Roadmap that enables them to get from where they are now to where they want to be.

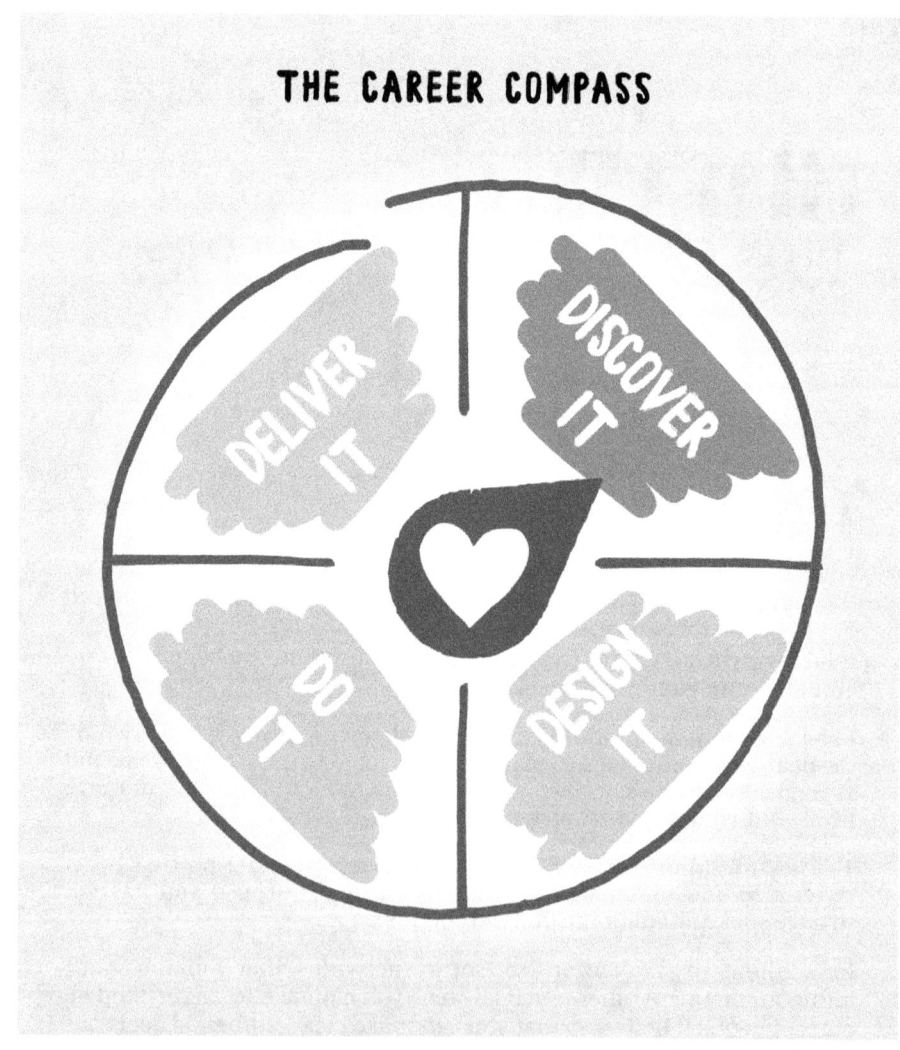

YOUR CAREER COMPASS – THE FOUR QUADRANTS

Your goal is to journey towards a career where you wake up every morning knowing that whatever circumstances life throws at you, you have the energy, resources, and commitment to face with courage and grace.

You've already acknowledged that the price of staying where you are is higher than the price of you doing the work to find what you want to do and a way to make it happen, so it's time to take a high-level view of the best tool you can use to guide your career journey from here as you follow the roadmap from where you are today, to where you want to be.

Let's start with the four quadrants. One of these quadrants will represent where you are today in your career cycle.

THE *DELIVER-IT* QUADRANT

This is the quadrant of your daily job. You may be considering aspects of one of the other quadrants, but your primary responsibility is to deliver what your employer expects and nail your existing role.

Your primary concerns in the *Deliver-It* Quadrant are:

1. **ACHIEVEMENT:** Being your best self and doing your best work. Achievement that is balanced with developing yourself toward your greatest potential.

2. **ATTITUDE:** Having a can-do, positive attitude towards your work to ensure you stand out and build a rock solid personal brand.

3. **ASSESSMENT:** Cultivating a strong sense of self-awareness at all stages of your career to ensure the most momentum, meaning and money.

THE *DISCOVER-IT* QUADRANT

In this quadrant you are discovering 'who you are'. What makes you tick and what is 'under your hood' of motivation, desires and needs. It's finding out how you are naturally wired, what you need and what you are great at.

The primary concerns in the *Discover-It* Quadrant are:

1. **IDENTITY:** What is your personality, your drivers, values and needs? What is your work style and what types of roles are you best suited to?

2. **INFLUENCERS:** Who and what influenced your past and current career decisions?

3. **INTERESTS:** What do you actually want to do? What are you good at, what do you like? What are your quests and causes? What are your chosen pathways?

THE DESIGN-IT QUADRANT

In this quadrant you will start the process of deliberately designing your career. You will think long term as well as short term. You will be thinking about what is next for you. You will identify any gaps in your skills, knowledge, beliefs, or actions that lie between where you are now and where you want to be. You will also design career goals in full alignment and clarity with who you are.

Your primary concerns in the *Design-It* Quadrant are:

1. **GOALS:** You will think about your career legacy and the eight different types of goals. You will think about safe, stretch and faith goals.

2. **GAPS:** Identification of skills and knowledge gaps between where you are now and where you want to be along with creation of 'what you want more of' in your career.

3. **GAME PLAN:** You will take the steps to map out your long, medium and short term action plans in alignment with your family, financial and creative goals.

THE DO-IT QUADRANT

Once you have discovered your Goals and Gaps and put together your Game Plan it's time to implement.

1. **POWER:** Level up with training and development and learn how to step into your own power with impact. Master your

mindset and nail skills like salary negotiation, personal branding and networking as you step up into your new role.

2. **POSITIONING:** Position yourself as an expert so opportunities come to you!

3. **PROMOTION:** You will target key people of influence and create specific, valuable messages about what you do to ensure you stand head and shoulders above your competition.

COMMON CAREER COMPASS MISTAKES.

1. Many people don't take the time to understand their career influences in the *Discover-It* Quadrant. This lack of self awareness is the reason why 80% of people unnecessarily change jobs and companies, as often this change is the result of a sudden feeling of disengagement: one day they are quite happy, then next they are ready to look at anything else. If you follow the advice and analysis I provide in the Career Navigators Roadmap Influences chapter, you'll find that you are well-equipped to diagnose the cause of your sudden disengagement which often comes down to a change in your core values or a sense that you are no longer growing or contributing as much as you need to, so your basic needs are no longer being met. If you are aware of this, there are often less drastic steps you can take to reignite your passion and purpose.

2. Another mistake is to jump straight into the *Do-It* Quadrant and start going for interviews and assessing roles based on whether you like the sound of them. This is the reverse of an effective strategy. You should start by considering what makes you tick, what you like, and don't like, and what career direction you want to pursue. In other words, you need to make conscious career decisions.

3. Regardless of your engagement level in the *Deliver-It* Quadrant it is important to consider the activities and planning in the *Discover-It* and *Design-It* Quadrants. You should assess this at least once a year, if not once a quarter. Part of your assessment in the *Deliver-It* Quadrant should be considering how you are tracking in your overall career as well as how you are feeling about your current role and alignment. You should think of having a mini-design in each of the quadrants and review them each quarter to ensure best results.

4. People leave positioning until they are ready to look for a new job. This is something that should be done all the time. Positioning is like your branding tool kit, it is your 'pull message' that provides the world with value and gives them a firm idea about who you are and what you stand for before they meet you.

5. Promotion needs to lose the negative connotation associated with 'selling yourself'. Yes, you are selling yourself and that is a good thing. Learning to connect with people, to communicate the value you are able to deliver to organisations and demonstrate the passion you have for particular ideas is incredibly powerful and inspirational. It's not cheesy and you should not be embarrassed to talk about yourself like that.

And so, a pathway appears in the form of this rockin' roadmap illustrated for you on the next page, to help you along the way. A step-by-step guide to take you from where you are to where you want to be and around again – you're welcome!

The Career Navigators Roadmap

THE ROADMAP

STEP 1

ACHIEVEMENT — YOUR CURRENT ROLE NAILED

IDENTITY — YOUR CAREER BLUEPRINT FOUND

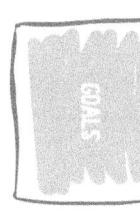 
GOALS — YOUR CAREER PLAN CREATED

POWER — YOUR CAREER GROWTH ACHIEVED

STEP 2

ATTITUDE

INFLUENCES

GAPS

POSITION

STEP 3

AWARENESS

INTERESTS

GAME PLAN

PROMOTE

Use this Roadmap to guide your journey through this next section. It is very closely related to the Career Compass, but not identical because the Roadmap is more linear. Since, at this point, we are setting you up with the foundations of your journey to an Epic Career, the linear approach is simpler because it ensures you cover each of the essential moving parts of your career.

The reality of your career is a little messier, more complex and more flexible, so it is also reflected by the circular diagram of the Career Compass which helps you see 'where you are'. Once you get your building blocks in place, it is an ongoing cycle of delivery, discovery, design, and doing to ensure that you stay aligned and self-aware.

Again this road map is much sexier in full colour so you can head to my website and download a bonus copy in full colour at my website at *www.rachelsparkes.com.au/resources*

This is where the rubber hits the road, and you come down to ground level and start to design a path forward. Most of my clients are amazed at how much more focused they are at developing new skills, and improving in the more challenging areas of their current roles when they have a clear path forward. That's why I spend so much time working through the 'Why' parts of your career, because when you are clear on your purpose, even the least congenial elements become easier

So, in the next section of the book we'll work through the Four Career Quadrants and the skills and techniques you can use to help you excel in each of them so that you can make progress in your journey through your Epic Career Quest.

1. **DELIVER-IT:** Doing a great job where you are now and achieving your company goals.

2. **DISCOVER-IT:** Identifying who you are, what drives you, and what you want to create so you can do what is right for you.

3. **DESIGN-IT:** Whole-Hearted connection and alignment to your goals and deliberate design of a career based on all that you are, so you are fully committed to the path ahead.

4. **DO-IT:** Improving and marketing yourself so that you connect and serve people in ways you have specifically identified to give you the greatest impact and choice.

THE DELIVER-IT QUADRANT

THE DELIVER-IT QUADRANT is where you will spend most of your time although you may also simultaneously be in other quadrants. It's the day-to-day quadrant of your job where you focus on delivering what you get paid to deliver by achieving goals and completing tasks for your organisation while also potentially earning bonuses, rewards, and other forms of recognition for your work. The Epic Career Quest is always about doing your best work, even in your current role, so in this quadrant we will be focusing on the following:

- Achievement
- Attitude
- Awareness

CHAPTER 8
ACHIEVEMENT

"If you neglect to recharge a battery it dies. And if you run full-speed ahead without stopping for water, you lose momentum to finish the race."
— Oprah Winfrey

OUR OBSESSION WITH DELIVERY

In today's modern work place almost every employee has a desire to achieve. The downside of achievement is that you are pulled in a variety of different directions. You are juggling the responsibility of delivering your company's goals and objectives along with building and managing your own career. If you're a leader then it gets even more challenging. You are probably responsible for recruiting and identifying top talent for your team, setting their objectives, and managing their performance to ensure they are on track. Then there are all the 'human' issues that pop up along the way... leave requests, personality conflicts, personal challenges... not to mention the actual work that you are supposed to produce to meet your own performance standards. People are working longer hours than ever before, and 'something's gotta give....'

What's giving is the resilience, productivity, and general wellbeing of staff. You can see it in the rise in burnout, the increase in sick days, staff turnover, and budget blowouts. Sound familiar? There is also a steady increase in employee disengagement on a global level. There is growing evidence that employee disengagement can be directly attributed to the failure to take development breaks throughout the year.

WHY BURNOUT IS SO COMMON

In today's competitive workplace the focus is on more efficient and more transparent delivery. However, research is showing that those who are not taking time out to engage in meaningful development activity are paying the price with their health. There is a growing body of literature across the fields of medicine and psychology that demonstrates that working harder, for longer without any real breaks to recharge can take a serious toll on your mental and physical health.

Breaks don't have to mean lying on a beach, though. According to study from Sweden's Uppsala University it's actually more effective for your mental health to learn or master a new skill. Yes, it's better to take a break to engage in a personal or professional development activity than to go on holidays!

The Finnish Institute of Occupational Health found that people who worked without a break were twice as likely to have a major depressive episode, even if they had no previous history of mental health issues. Another study reviewed 50 years of research published by the American Journal of Epidemiology. It showed that working non-stop with no scheduled breaks increased the risk of coronary heart disease by 80% in both sexes. The researchers reasoned that the correlation may be related in part to health problems associated with longer exposure to psychological stress.

So make sure you head to that course, go on that conference or hire that coach to develop yourself. It's not only good for your pay packet but it's good for your general wellbeing too. Reframing the way we look at achievement means that we include personal and professional development within the mix, instead of narrowly focusing on the end result. Think of achievement more holistically as a balance of momentum and meaning as well as a balance of input (development) and output (delivery).

CHAPTER 9
YOUR ATTITUDE

"I am not what's happened to me. I am what I choose to become."
- Carl Jung

If you have worked in any corporate environment for any period of time you will start to see that one of the major challenges is dealing with the people you work with. You may or may not be aware but if you want to be a true game changer in your career then it starts with absolutely nailing your current role. One of the key ingredients to doing this and beginning the foundation of a rock solid personal brand is to have a killer attitude.

What do I mean by killer attitude? I mean a positive, enthusiastic and committed attitude towards your work, co-workers, leaders and wider organisation. I'm not saying you have to drink the Kool-Aid and sell your soul but I am saying that a good attitude goes a long way.

Take a look at the model over the page to see where you fit.

ATTITUDE AWARENESS

```
                    POSITIVE RESULTS
                  |
        HIDE      |      STAND
         OUT      |       OUT
                  |
NEGATIVE ATTITUDE ————————————————— POSITIVE ATTITUDE
                  |
        MOVE      |       CALL
         OUT      |        OUT
                  |
                    NEGATIVE RESULTS
```

YOU STAND OUT

This is where you have both a positive attitude and are getting positive results in your career. A good place to be! You are a Stand Out person and are being noticed. Your brand is being set on a solid foundation and you are well liked and positioned for future roles and opportunities.

YOU CALL OUT

This is where you have a fantastic attitude but you are not getting the results you desire. So you call out the training or support you need to get there. You may or may not be aware of the obstacle that stands in your way but you are enthusiastic enough to try to overcome it.

YOU HIDE OUT

This is where you get the job done, you make the sales or get the product out the door but you have a stinking attitude. You 'hide out' under the radar with your results. You are probably not well liked and you are probably difficult to work with. You don't like being part of the team, you are resistant and can be toxic. The sad thing is you are probably miserable and you could be doing so much more with yourself.

YOU MOVE OUT

This is where you have both a stinking attitude and poor results. It's everybody else's fault except your own. You whine, complain, and gossip. You are lazy and cause more problems than actual outcomes for your company. It's probably best you move out of the organisation or I guarantee you they will be devising a plan to move you out! You need to change your attitude and get the skills and support to change.

WHAT IS A STAND OUT ATTITUDE?

After interviewing 10,000 or so people and hearing all their 'horror stories' of colleagues and leaders that were doing their head in, I have compiled a list of what it means to have a positive attitude at work.

HAVING A CAN DO ATTITUDE: Now this doesn't mean that you are a doormat always saying yes to everything. You have strong boundaries and understand your capacity but you approach ideas, requests and new projects with excitement and vigor. You don't give up and do think anything is possible. If road blocks appear you communicate and find solutions early.

BEING RESPECTFUL TO OTHERS: Whether it's a passive aggressive co-worker who makes your life hell, or a sleazy manager who makes inappropriate comments about your clothes or make up, or a boss who demeans you and takes the credit for your work in a meeting, don't be like those people. Just be mindful of others by giving credit where it's due, respecting boundaries and celebrating the achievements of the team.

BEING CARING: Being caring in the workplace shouldn't be a foreign concept. We are all humans with lives, families, stories and emotions. We are not robots or pretend versions of ourselves when we walk through the office doors. Take off the mask and realise that part of being a stand out is having genuine care for others, and genuine care for your customers. And don't forget your suppliers. They are people too.

HAVING A TRANSPARENT WORK ETHIC: After working in the recruitment and software sales industry for nearly two decades I am still amazed at how easy it is for sales people to 'hide' their true activity in elaborate stories about big deals and pipelines that never seem to materialise. The best most memorable and successful sales people are totally transparent about their activity, their failures and successes. Leaders are the same. If you are transparent about your work, you will be much more successful in your career.

HAVING A PROBLEM SOLVING APPROACH: As a HR consultant I would get many people asking to speak to me about issues around the work place. I learnt to give them about 10 minutes of my time to tell me the issue and would always ask them what they would like me to do about it. 100% of the time they never had an answer. I asked them to go away and think about 2 - 3 potential solutions before they came to me again. Then we would discuss the best way forward. As an employee and consultant whenever I approach someone with a potential problem I always state the problem but provide 2 - 3 potential solutions and the ideal outcome for all parties. Do the thinking, don't be another problem - attempt to solve it yourself.

BEING COLLABORATIVE: Working well in teams and sharing your ideas and delegating are all part of great collaboration. Having a great attitude towards others and not always needing control is part of being a stand out inside organisations.

BEING SUPPORTIVE OF NEW IDEAS AND INNOVATION: Shutting people down for raising ideas out of their 'turn' or 'position' is not going to get you anywhere. Sure, that one idea may have been a stinker but you want to be someone who people will come to with ideas whether you're a leader, an expert or a business owner. You never know when a genius idea will arrive and how it may help you and your career.

OWNING UP TO AND LEARNING FROM MISTAKES: When you screw something up, own it. It will build respect and trust with your leaders and co-workers so much more than hiding it. Realise that when you fail or make a mistake, you are human and the quickest road to redemption is actually admitting you made a mistake.

TELLING THE TRUTH: If you can't deliver on time, just say you can't then work out the best possible scenario. If you don't want to work on a project because you can't stand someone, just tell the truth and if you are a leader and someone is not getting where they should in their career because they are an annoying twat - then tell them. Furthermore, if you are a business owner and want to sell your company - tell your staff. Instead of hiding it, it could be the most exciting vision to get them on board. The truth will always set you free.

CHAPTER 10
YOUR AWARENESS

Self-awareness is not self-centeredness, and spirituality is not narcissism. 'Know thyself' is not a narcissistic pursuit.

- Marianne Williamson

Self-Awareness is an essential skill to keep in mind as you absolutely nail your current role. You need to remain aware of how you are doing and feeling, and how others perceive your performance. At the start of your Epic Career Quest, you are possibly uninspired by your current position, but hang in there and work at delivering with excellence, because things are about to change.

According to the book, *Life Changing Self Awareness: Empowering Education and Career Growth*, by Kelvin Batten, self-awareness is a major component of emotional intelligence (EQ). When you understand yourself, you are one step closer to understanding others... and this plays a critical role in your success.

You know those 'babushka dolls', where you open one layer after another until you get to the tiny heart of the doll? Your search for self-awareness in your career path is like your journey to the heart of the doll. The outside layers are your existing skills, knowledge and experience. As you open each layer of the doll you see the things that are uniquely you - your values, personality, interests and talents - and at the centre you find your inner, guiding self.

YOUR CHARGE INDICATOR

One of the biggest parts of self-awareness is how engaged or happy you are in your current role. You may get asked about this in an 'employee engagement' survey but how often do you check in with yourself on a monthly, weekly or daily basis?

I have created The 'Charge Indicator Tool' below to diagnose your level of charge (like the charge on your phone battery) at any stage in your career. Think of charge as your level of happiness or engagement. It is particularly helpful in the Deliver-IT Quadrant, because your level of charge is one of your self-awareness tools, and will affect your performance in the job, and your ability to position yourself for future opportunities. You may find some 'quick fix' solutions to help you continue to nail your existing position as you think through other areas of your life and future direction.

THE CHARGE INDICATOR TOOL

	DEVELOPMENT	NO DEVELOPMENT	
ALIGNED	SUPER CHARGED ZONE	BURNOUT ZONE (TIME TO RECHARGE)	
NOT ALIGNED	ROBOT ZONE (TIME TO RECONNECT)	FLAT ZONE	

#1: THE SUPER CHARGED ZONE

Imagine that you have just started in a new role. You are fully charged, fully energised, and fully aligned with your role. You are totally dedicated to doing a great job and are supported by your managers. This is the Super Charged Zone. Ideally, you (and most of your colleagues) would spend most of your time here.

Interestingly, research shows that when people return from significant and interesting development activity, and feel their personal career goals are in alignment with company objectives, they also function in this zone.

#2: THE BURN OUT ZONE

At some point your engagement will peak. This may be when the effect of your development activity wears off and you move into a space where you are no longer growing, but are still aligned with the company objectives. At this stage, the constant focus on delivery and performance starts to deplete your battery charge. You start to feel overwhelmed and unmotivated. If you don't take action, you could soon end up in the Flat Zone.

#3: THE FLAT ZONE

A burnt out employee will eventually end up in the Flat Zone: switched off and potentially even destructive. You will not engage in development activity and you will feel emotionally (and often physically) burnt out and unaligned with the company objectives.

At this point, your manager may sense there is a problem and send you on a course to try and keep you happy for a while. This will just be a temporary fix - it is essential to address your lack of alignment as quickly as possible so you don't end up in the Robot Zone just going through the motions out of a sense of obligation.

#4: THE ROBOT ZONE

You may already be functioning in this zone, since I know that you are looking for a more satisfying career, but the reality is, it can strike at any stage if you are not careful. If you're in the Robot Zone your performance is neither destructive nor amazing. You do what is required in your job and get by, but you have no passion or emotional engagement with what you do. Those around you probably feel that you are just in your role to pay the bills and fill in time. Even if you are engaged in development activity, since you are not in alignment with your company objectives you will probably oscillate between the Robot Zone and the Flat Zone.

It's very difficult to realign yourself to an organisation's objectives once you lose that alignment. This is why you need to consider alignment very carefully when evaluating and seeking opportunities. If your values aren't aligned with those of your organisation you will quickly slide into the Robot Zone once you become familiar with your tasks.

THE DISCOVER-IT QUADRANT

THE DISCOVER-IT Quadrant is the quadrant where you start thinking about what might be your next steps or further goals. This is where you explore your dreams for the future and everything that you want to achieve. Ideally, you will design your short-term, medium-term, and long-term career goals in full alignment and clarity with who you are. You will also identify any gaps that exist in your skills, knowledge, beliefs, or actions that might prevent you from achieving your dreams, as well as any other obstacles that might stand in your way.

The Epic Career Quest is about really knowing 'who you are' so in this quadrant we will focus on the following:

- Your Identity
- Your Influences
- Your Interests

CHAPTER 11
YOUR IDENTITY

"Your personality is more than a thing you can measure in a lab – it's about your heart and soul."
— Carl Jung

YOUR CAREER BLUEPRINT MODEL

Your Career Blueprint summarises 'who you are' in your career. It incorporates your identity, influences, and interests... all the things that make you uniquely you and help you find joy in your career. In order to find the greatest amount of fulfilment, impact, and joy in your career, you will want to use this tool as the primary filter. At the heart of your Career Blueprint is your Career Sweet Spot, the intersecting area where your identity, influences, and interests are most strongly evident. This is where you will find the most aligned roles and the greatest satisfaction.

When you are in the Career Sweet Spot, it's like having the perfect wheel alignment for your vehicle. If your wheels are out of alignment your tyres get worn down quickly and it's hard to steer in the right direction. However, when your wheels are in perfect alignment it's easy to control your vehicle and travel smoothly toward your destination.

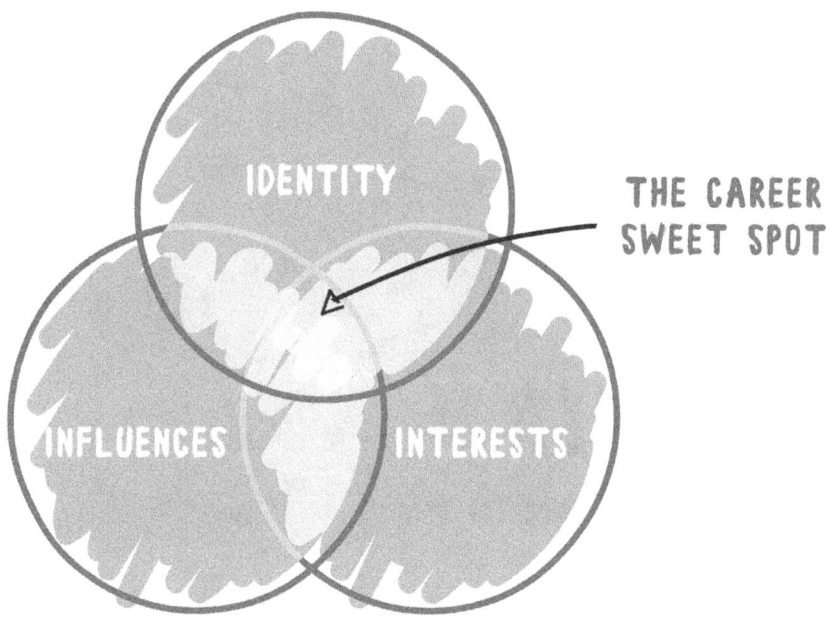

You can achieve your Career Sweet Spot when you align these three key parts of yourself with your position:-

1. **Identity:** How you are wired.
2. **Interests:** What you are good at.
3. **Influences:** What's important to you.

CASE STUDY

ON THE CAREER SWEET SPOT

Jane* came to see me because she did not know 'where to start' with her career planning. She was a brand manager in a finance business but she was feeling dissatisfied and ready to move. As she considered her next career step, she wanted to think about more than just her skills, knowledge, and abilities.

Once we discussed other factors and she expanded her self-awareness to include aspects such as her personality, values, interests, work environment preferences, and her unique strengths and motivators she had a far more holistic view of what she enjoyed and where she wanted her career to take her. As a result she created a career design that has brought much more joy and meaning to her life than one which was based on her skills and knowledge alone. As she said to me, "If I hadn't taken the time to work through all the other aspects of who I am I would probably have bounced around every few years when I felt unhappy at work. After working with you, I not only know myself better, but am able to assess offers more quickly and easily (and ignore most of them)."

---

*Names have been changed to protect privacy

YOUR CAREER PERSONALITY

According to the dictionary your identity or personality is the combination of characteristics or qualities that form your distinctive character. The well-known psychologist, Carl Gustav Jung (1875-1961), founder of Analytic Psychology, and Jungian Psychology, proposed that there are eight personality types based on opposing attitudes of introversion and extroversion. According to his definition, attitudes refer to a predisposition to behave in a certain manner. People who are classified as introverts place importance on their subjective view of the world, while extroverts place more emphasis on objectivity and surrounding influences. Jung further identified four functions of the personality: feeling, thinking, sensation, and intuition. Feeling and thinking refer to the rational thought processes that allow us to understand the value and meaning of things. Sensation and intuition are non-rational functions by which we perceive the world - either through our sense organs (sensation), or by means of an unconscious process (intuition). These four functions and two attitudes combine to create eight distinct personality types: extroverted-thinking, introverted-thinking, extroverted-feeling, introverted-feeling, extroverted-sensing, introverted-sensing, extroverted-intuitive, and introverted-intuitive.

These same personality types formed the basis of the sixteen personalities of the Myers-Briggs Type Indicator (MBTI), the world's most widely used personality assessment tool, which is used to determine how a person perceives the world and makes decisions. As part of your holistic career personality discovery I strongly recommend completing a Myers-Briggs Type Indicator (MBTI) personality assessment to understand specifically how you perceive the world and make your career decisions.

In the case of your career, your personality or identity often sways your judgement of situations and influences how you deal with people and tasks. According to Jung, the idea is to first understand your 'wiring' and then work out how best you can work with what you have. What was really interesting to me was that in exploring his system of personality types Jung relied as much on observation as on formal case data. This means he didn't just survey hundreds or thousands of people in clinical trials to get the data on the MBTI personality types. This work that spanned 20 years was based on the countless impressions and experiences derived from the treatment of nervous illnesses, from interactions with people of all social levels, and from an analysis of his own psychological nature.

I found this deeply inspiring as, while I have a deep respect for research and clinical trialling, Jung's book is rich in material drawn from literature, religion, and philosophy. I love his ultimate analysis that what makes up your personality is more than a thing you can measure in a lab - it's about the heart and soul of a person.

CHARACTERS AND IDENTITY EXPRESSIONS

In addition to the Jungian or MBTI personality types, the character and identity expression tool is another helpful way of looking at yourself and understanding how you are wired. The dictionary defines 'character' as the aggregate of features and traits that form the individual nature of some person or thing. So you can think of it like this, your personality is how you are wired to think about the world and make decisions, while your character is your primary nature, which is made up of multiple identity expressions. This primary nature is expressed through the way in which you act, behave and do things.

Your character and identity expressions have both positive and negative qualities. Once you are aware of these expressions of yourself, you can choose which ones to express.

I developed the following 20 Characters and Identity Expressions for your career personality over the course of interviewing 10,000 plus candidates. As I listened to their description of what they were looking for in their future careers I started to collate the words they used to describe what they wanted more of, or ways they wanted to express themselves, and I noticed an interesting emerging pattern. There were certain words that were usually grouped together in threes. These three verbs were closely linked to particular character traits they exhibited. When I started feeding these characters back to candidates their eyes would light up as they identified the parts of their personality they wanted to grow, or tap into, or start to express in the future.

Work It Real Good - Rachel Sparkes

HOW TO IDENTIFY YOUR CURRENT CHARACTER AND IDENTITY EXPRESSIONS

1. Read through the list of characters and the short descriptions below.

2. Pick the three that immediately resonate with you. The ones that make you think, "Yes, this is who I am!"

3. Then pick two more that you think exist under your skin, that want to come out but don't have any outlet.

4. Then pick two others that you would like to minimise (negative expressions).

IDENTITY EXPRESSIONS WITHIN A PERSONALITY

	THE CHARACTER	THE BEHAVIOR		
1	THE LOVER	CARING	INTIMACY	AFFECTION
2	THE SAINT	KINDNESS	HELPING	CONTRIBUTION
3	THE STUDENT	LEARN	EXPLORE	GROW
4	THE MASTER	TEACH	GUIDE	MENTOR
5	THE ACHIEVER	EFFICIENT	EFFECTIVE	RESOURCEFUL
6	THE BOSS	COMPETENT	CAPABLE	CONFIDENT
7	THE MAKER	PRODUCE	CREATE	INNOVATE
8	THE CONNECTOR	SOCIALISE	VOLUNTEER	BELONG
9	THE ATHLETE	NOURISH	EXERCISE	MEDITATE
10	THE CONTROLLER	ORDERED	STRUCTURED	POWERFUL
11	THE REBEL	SPONTANEOUS	FLEXIBLE	RELAXED
12	THE CUSTOMER	SPECTATE	CONSUME	PURCHASE
13	THE HEALER	DIAGNOSE	PRESCRIBE	COUNSEL
14	THE VICTIM	BLAME	COMPLAIN	MANIPULATE
15	THE DESTROYER	HARM	ABUSE	DEMEAN
16	THE DEVIL	LIE	CHEAT	STEAL
17	THE CHILD	PLAYFUL	TRUSTING	ENERGETIC
18	THE PARENT	PROTECTION	RESPONSIBILITY	STRENGTH
19	THE CARER	FEED	CLEAN	CLOTHE
20	THE CHEERLEADER	SUPPORT	ENCOURAGE	BELIEVE

THE CHARACTER DESCRIPTIONS

Now check out the short descriptions below for each of the characters in this grid.

1. **THE LOVER:** Your identity is focused on giving. Your intention and actions are based on serving and loving. You care about others, the community, and the environment. You crave intimacy and affection with the people you work and live with. You put others before yourself.

2. **THE SAINT:** Your identity is focused on serving. You are always kind and see the best in people. You think about how you can help others. You actively contribute to the community and environment.

3. **THE STUDENT:** Your identity is focused on learning. You desire to grow and expand. To learn and explore new things. To push yourself outside of your comfort zone and be around inspiring people and situations that are able to challenge you.

4. **THE MASTER:** Your identity is focused on teaching. You desire to pay it forward and give to those who come after you. You want to guide and mentor those who need to tap into the wisdom you have learned as you followed your own unique path.

5. **THE ACHIEVER:** Your identity is focused on manifesting. You use the power of your mind and the universe to become more efficient and effective at what you do. You create inspired, innovative ideas about how to make things happen and get to new places. You identify and collate resources in people and your physical environment to manifest your desires, ideas, and projects.

6. **THE BOSS:** Your identity is focused on leadership. You are competent, trustworthy and capable of making decisions. You are confident in your visions, your people, and yourself.

7. **THE MAKER:** Your identity is focused on creativity. You produce new things based on your thoughts, ideas, and emotions. You use innovative processes to bring your ideas to life.

8. **THE CONNECTOR:** Your identity is focused on relationships. You care about people and truly want them to succeed. You socialise and put others in touch with people who can help with their personal growth. You give your time and energy to people and take the time to immerse yourself in the communities you choose to invest in.

9. **THE ATHLETE:** Your identity is focused on health and wellbeing. You feed your body healthy food, exercise on a regular basis and nourish your mind with meditation to continue your spiritual growth.

10. **THE CONTROLLER:** Your identity is focused on either your own power-based ego or in the desire to co-ordinate others. You are ordered, organised, and structured. You have the power but must be careful not to want the power for its own sake, as this motivation is based on fear.

11. **THE REBEL:** Your identity can be focused on reckless abandon or conscious revolution. Some rules should be broken, but rules that are broken without conscious awareness could be destructive for you and others. The rebel is spontaneous and has difficulty fitting within the confines of normal expectations. They can be relaxed and flexible. They can also be unreliable and lazy, but with the right intention the rebel expression can change the world for the better.

12. **THE CUSTOMER:** Your identity is focused on experience. You enjoy being a spectator at events and you engage in the financial economy by consuming and purchasing things. Consuming and experience can be positive and necessary, but if used to fill a gap in your spirit, to impress others or for ego-centric status, general mindless consumerism can be destructive to you and the planet.

13. **THE HEALER:** You express this identity centred on your intention of restoration. Whether it's an old house, a financial budget, a leadership program to change culture, healing the planet or a person, you can see the potential in anything to be fully alive, functioning, and beautiful. You can diagnose the problems, prescribe remedies and provide counsel on the solutions.

14. **THE VICTIM:** Your identity is focused on gaining attention and validation for your pain rather than learning from it or moving away from it. Uncomfortable emotions, and unpleasant or unwanted situations are never your fault. You take no responsibility for any part of it and you blame others in order to shift the pain away from yourself. You complain about every aspect of your life, career, and relationships. You can be capricious and may hold other people responsible for your decisions and ultimate happiness.

15. **THE DESTROYER:** You express this identity with your intention focused on control and fear, ultimately you want to put others down so you can rise to the top. You probably don't set out to do this, but you find yourself causing harm to people and things around you whether that is the company culture, the project, the environment. You frequently demean people and 'put them in their place'. You like others to feel shame and guilt. You find yourself saying mean things about people behind their backs and fuelling gossip about others.

16. **THE DEVIL:** Your identity is focused on concealing the truth and gaining advantages for yourself. Whether the lie is small and white, or big and black you use 'untruthful' information or conversation to gain advantage. You cut corners and cheat your colleagues and clients out of a fair and honourable exchange of value. You steal ideas, information, and even potentially physical property without remorse because you feel entitled to it all.

17. **THE CHILD:** Your identity is focused on wonder and trust. You approach situations with playfulness, curiosity, and excitement. You have an innate trust in your environment and the people around you. You have boundless energy to overcome problems and try new things. You respect boundaries when set by caring people who genuinely care about your growth.

18. **THE PARENT:** Your identity is focused on stimulating growth in those around you. You seek to protect others and provide situations and environments where they can learn and grow. You take responsibility for the care and growth of others. You set boundaries and guide people to the right choices while making them feel strong and secure. You represent strength either physically, emotionally, or culturally to those around you.

19. **THE CARER:** Your identity is focused on serving others. You spend your time nursing, caring, feeding, clothing and even cleaning for others. You provide and create environments where people feel safe and nurtured.

20. **THE CHEERLEADER:** Your identity is focused on supporting others. You spend your time listening to others, encouraging them to push themselves to be their best and helping them believe in themselves.

THE STOP LIGHT GUIDE

Now that you have identified the characters that best describe you, your second step is to consider which character traits are serving you and which are not serving you (or others). The Stop Light Guide on the next page shows that traits have either a positive or a negative energy. Some traits are based on giving out to others, others focus on taking (or receiving).

Character traits in the Red Light area are cause for alarm. There are three character traits that are clearly negative and don't help anyone - the destroyer, the devil and the victim. If you recognise yourself in any of these, now may be a good time to think about how to stop doing or behaving in those ways and start to identify with a more beneficial character trait that helps you and others.

If you have identified with a Yellow Light character then you can proceed with caution. The controller, the boss, the achiever, the child, the rebel and the customer are all give or take, positive or negative. Depending on your intentions these identity expressions can be positive or negative. The key is to practice great self-awareness in these expressions.

The Green Light expressions are all systems go! They are generally full of positive energy and focused on both giving and receiving in a way that serves you and others. The Saint, The Healer, The Carer, The Master, The Parent, The Cheerleader, The Maker, The Athlete, The Connector, The Student and The Lover. If you express your identity here you are probably making good decisions as your intention is coming from a place of intuition and love.

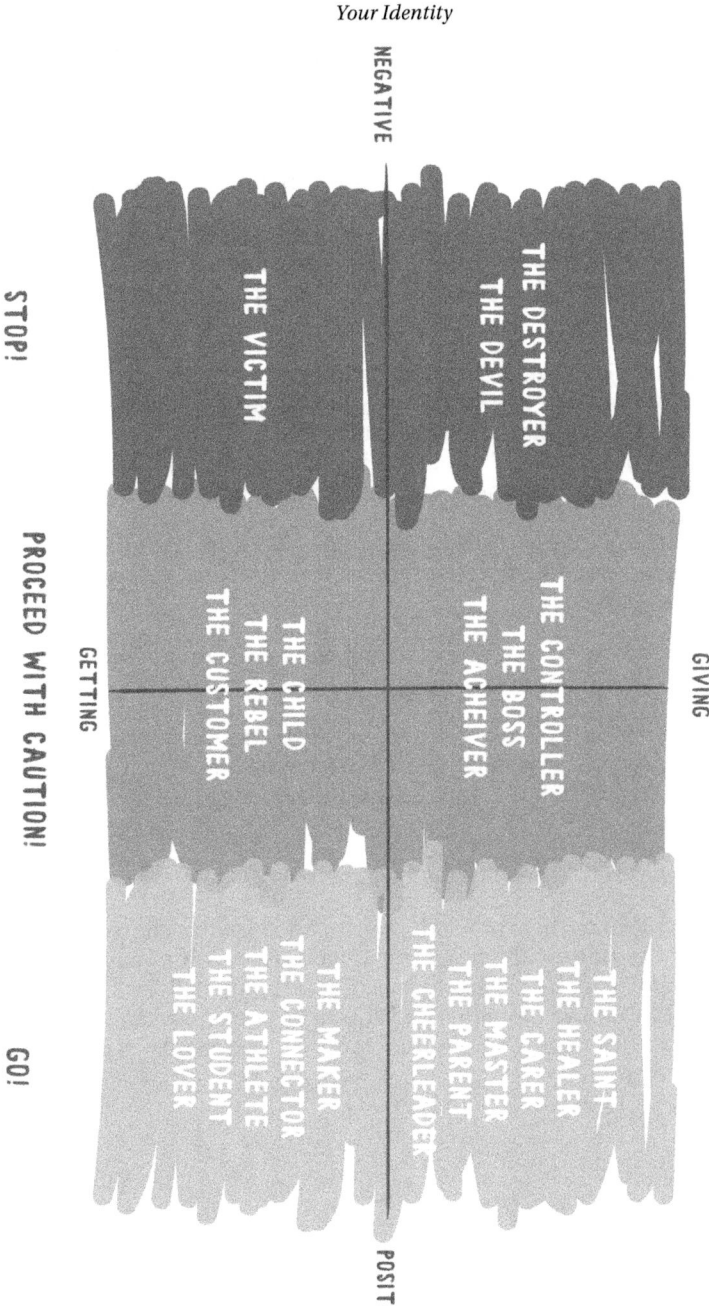

When I talk about these characters and identity expressions with clients I commonly get asked whether they really can change the things they do. I'm always reminded of a fabulous story about the balance of human nature. Picture the Yin and the Yang: there is always a balance of light and darkness in all of us. This is a picture of our potential not our reality.

The darkness represents our negative emotions such as fear, anger, envy, greed, regret, self-pity, and guilt. We may experience it as resentment or feelings of inferiority or superiority. It causes us to lie or to feel a false sense of pride.

On the other side, the light represents love. We experience it as feelings of joy, peace and hope. We see it in all our positive desires like our generosity, our quest for truth, our compassion and our faith in ourselves and others as well as our feelings of serenity and our ability to be humble, kind, accept others and show true empathy.

So, the question remains, "If all these potential expressions are in me, how do I ensure that the right ones are expressed?" The answer is given in a beautiful proverb:

A student monk sat meditating on the balance of light and dark in all humans. Perplexed he came to his guru and asked him this question:

"Inside of me there are two dogs. One is mean and filled with fear and hate and the other is good and holds my creative and loving potential. They fight each other all the time. In the battle of my life, which dog will win?"

The guru answered, "The one you feed the most."

Inside each one of us there are both positive and negative characteristics, and we are the ones with the power to choose which to express. We make this choice by becoming aware of our thoughts, identifying the emotion behind those thoughts, and then by consciously choosing our actions since these are the building blocks of the identity expressions and characters.

CASE STUDY:
TAKING RESPONSIBILITY FOR YOUR GROWTH

Jessica* is a university lecturer and wants to ensure that her career goals are fully aligned with her personality. She works through the Character-Identity tool and recognises that her identity is most aligned to:-

THE MASTER: She is a teacher and already guides her students. She decides to put her hand up for the university mentoring program to extend this aspect of her life.

THE REBEL: Her university life enables her to be flexible and relaxed in her approach to life. She thinks of ways to be more spontaneous in her lecturing.

THE ACHIEVER: She is already efficient and effective in her work but often finds that she can't do everything herself. She decides to outsource some of her work and discover ways to be more resourceful.

Jessica also identifies some characteristics that want to come out but are not currently being expressed:-

THE BOSS: She is competent and capable but often lacks self-confidence so she doesn't put up her hand for leadership roles.

THE SAINT: She realises that she is not expressing kindness, helping, or contributing much in her work or life in general. She looks for ways to be part of a charity so that she can donate her time to the organisation. She also thinks about how she can be more helpful and kind in her daily work.

Jessica then also recognises some traits that are not serving her.

THE CHILD: She recognises that she can be a bit naïve and vulnerable to office politics. She decides to take an emotional intelligence course as well as some training on how to have difficult conversations.

THE VICTIM: She acknowledges that when things go wrong she tends to blame others. She starts to think about being more accountable in her work.

As time goes on, Jessica instinctively acts more and more in line with the characters she has chosen to nurture.

*Names have been changed to protect privacy

CHAPTER 12
YOUR INFLUENCES

"Your true self is always motivated by love, not fear."

- Rachel Sparkes

Who or What was behind your Past Career Decisions?

The purpose of this self-check-in and background review is to identify your main career motivators from the past. It's amazing how many people discover that their life today is shaped by people and circumstances in the past that are no longer relevant. This understanding can be incredibly freeing as you realise that you now have the power to change your choices.

In his book, *What Happy People Know,* Dr. Dan Baker says that in the ultimate analysis of behavior in human beings there are only two primal motives: fear and love. Fear compels us to survive, and love enables us to thrive. Therefore, it's important to find out if your career decisions are motivated primarily by fear or by love.

If your core career motivation is based on fear, then no matter how successful you are, at the end of your career you will still be unfulfilled and unhappy. You will always be striving for something more and seeking something else to fill the void that your fear creates inside you. On the other hand, if your career motivation is based on love for what you do, then you will find satisfaction every day (even amidst the frustrations) and you will be able to celebrate your successes before passing onto your next goal.

Once you identify your core motivations and influences, you can decide whether they still serve you and let them go if they don't. Once you know that your motivations and intentions are coming from the right place you will have clarity and conviction as you deliberately design your career.

So, I'd like you to ask yourself who or what shaped your choice of career. You may know immediately, or you may have to think for a while, but you should be able to come up with 3-5 influencers.

CASE STUDY

THE POWER OF EXTERNAL INFLUENCES

One of my private clients was aware of a nagging emptiness and persistent dissatisfaction with his career in the advertising industry. He realised that he had chosen his career in advertising because he felt it was what he 'ought to do', and would provide good money and many opportunities for advancement. His decision was heavily influenced by his private school upbringing and the expectations he had learned.

He was blown away to discover that he had chosen his career based on these external influences and to realise how much power they still had over him. Once he became aware of his motivations he was free to make new career decisions, and today he is taking a course in remedial massage. His new energy and enthusiasm for life more than compensates for the changes his family has made and they could not be happier with that decision.

DISCOVER YOUR EMOTIONAL CATALYSTS

If you have ever done any form of Cognitive Behavioural Therapy or read anything by Sigmund Freud you will understand the concept that a lot of your adult behaviour is shaped by an emotional response to major events in your childhood.

This principle is certainly true for your career motivations. One career coach in the USA gets all of his clients to write down seven events they had an emotional reaction to that had an effect on their career. I find that usually just one or two events from your early childhood and one or two events from your high school years is just as effective in exposing the emotional catalysts behind your career decisions. These influences may be major, like death, disease, divorce, or a major accident, or they could be apparently trivial events like wearing the wrong clothes to a party, or forgetting your lines in the school play, or not having the right sneakers. It doesn't matter what they are, the important thing is the emotional impact they had on you.

These emotional catalysts can secretly influence your ongoing career decisions in ways that do not serve you or they may be a positive influence, but the important thing is that you want to be aware of them, you don't want them to be a secret influence!

Think of what drives you now and go back to the time when your belief or motivation was born. Who or what was it that began it all?

Ultimately my learning from this is that there is nothing 'wrong' with being motivated and driven to succeed by fear, it can even produce positive results. But at some point your motivation needs to change. If you are not acting out of love, then love cannot exist. At some point I needed to accept the life and experience that was behind me, be grateful for all the lessons I learned, see it for the abundance and treasure it was, and then turn my perception of it around. I'm not afraid anymore, and I'm not running away from anything. The propulsion of the fear, the fire in my belly to get away from my perceived lack was enough for a while but it wasn't everlasting or eternal like love.

DISCOVER YOUR CIRCLE OF INFLUENCERS

A sneaky influencer that is often perceived as healthy is 'competition'. Matt Church, founder of the Thought Leaders' Business School, says the killer of all creativity is comparison. I think this is the very real danger posed by Facebook and Instagram and other social media sites where we are constantly and subtly urged to compare ourselves with others.

When we compare ourselves with others, our self-talk brings up all sorts of untrue ideas about where the other person is in their life and where we are in comparison. It's a recipe for disaster! This is a game you will never win and it's all based on ego.

Check in with yourself by writing down the names of all your VIPs - your Very Important People. These are the people in your life who are your true friends and family. They genuinely care about you and would put your needs and growth before their own. If you were considering a career change you would confide in your VIPs, but they would ultimately encourage and trust you to make your own decisions.

In reality, no-one other than your VIPs should have any influence over your career decisions. However, other people and other groups of people do creep in from time to time. Have you ever caught yourself wondering, "What would 'people' think if I went back to work when my child was only six months old?" Or perhaps you're thinking, "When Cathy (whom I haven't seen since high school) sees that I'm working at PWC on my Facebook status she'll be really impressed." We all do it from time to time, the idea is to catch yourself when you are comparing yourself with others, or trying to impress someone, so that you make your career decisions based on who you are, not on outside influences.

I have a good friend who has generously allowed me to use his story in this book. When I first started my coaching practice he was coming to speak to me in a 'frentoring' capacity. I had a lot of respect for him as he was a legal advisor and had helped me a lot with my earlier recruitment business. We are very similar in how we approach 'doing what you love' for a career.

It was obvious that he was growing unhappy with his work as a consulting lawyer so I asked if he would like to be a guinea pig for some of the tools I was developing for my coaching practice.

We met for about three hours and dived deep into many of his career influencers. We identified the following:

VIP's - spouse, family and friends who he listens to.

CARS - Colleagues, Associates, and Relatives he sees regularly, but who are not VIP's.

GROUPS - ethnic groups, business groups, religious groups he is a part of

SOCIETY - wider community, country etc.

Then we looked more closely at each group and considered whether any of these groups had influenced his past or current career decisions. What we found out was astounding.

He had decided to become a lawyer because that's what many of his peers and career guidance counsellors said he should do. He also felt that his parents and the school system had encouraged him to pursue a 'status oriented' profession. More recently he was thinking of purchasing a Porsche - just for show! Ever since high school he had done 'that thing': working in a job you hate, to buy things you don't need, to impress people you don't even like. This was a hard realisation, since he was in his mid-40s, used to the identity and status that his job and income had given him and suddenly he had some truths and potential changes to face.

The good news is that over the past few years he has transitioned to a much better career situation. He consults part time for a renewable energy venture capital firm that he is passionate about. He also has entrepreneurial 'fingers in the pie' with large wind farm projects as well as some social networking and wine projects in the pipeline.

Coaching Questions for Your Influencers

☐ What or who have most of the decisions to take or move to different jobs been influenced by?

☐ Were these decisions ultimately made by me, or overly influenced by others?

☐ At what point did I become the primary influencer in my career plans and decisions?

☐ Do I feel confident in making my current career plans and decisions?

☐ If I were to make career changes who would support me whole heartedly?

☐ Do I compete with anyone that does not serve me?

☐ Am I trying to impress anyone that does not serve me?

☐ Am I influenced by family or friends who may have good intentions but have their own agenda?

☐ How can I make decisions from now on that serve me and allow me to step into my own power?

YOUR VALUES ARE WHAT YOU NEED

People are not the only influencers on our careers. We are also driven by our own intrinsic values. Values can be defined as what you need in your career. This can be an ambiguous term and different people value different things, but, as Roy Disney said, "It's not hard to make your decisions once you know what your values are." I like to keep it simple and define a value as something that you need and that is important to you. Once you understand what you need, then you can easily define your values and understand how they influence your decisions.

According to Anthony Robbins, there are six fundamental needs that exist in every person and you must take them all into account when considering your career. When you get these six fundamentals right it's like eating a balanced diet. You feel energised, fuelled, and ready for anything that comes toward you.

The six fundamental needs are:-

1. **CHALLENGE:** The need for growth, development and expansion. Some people need constant challenge, other people prefer to stick with the familiar and like a high degree of repetition;

2. **CONNECTION:** The need to work with others and feel part of a team. People with a high need for connection enjoy group projects, meetings, and environments where they spend a lot of time communicating with others;

3. **RECOGNITION:** The need to be rewarded and acknowledged for what they do. People with a high need for recognition love titles, certificates, and awards ceremonies, the more public the better, but we all have a need for affirmation in what we do;

4. **SECURITY:** The need for certainty and continuity. People with a high need for security can really struggle in the present organisational environment because of the constant change and rumour. These people would love to start their career straight out of university and stay with the same company until they retire.

5. **GROWTH:** As humans we have an innate need to grow. When you are not growing in your role, you start to feel bored and disengaged. No one really wants to operate on auto-pilot. We love to be stretched and to extend our current thinking and abilities. We are happiest at work when we are challenged because that is when we grow.

6. **CONTRIBUTION:** At some point our values and needs are connected to contribution. This doesn't necessarily mean 'altruistic' contribution. It simply means that what you do makes a real difference in some way. For example, think about the person on an IT help desk. If they are busy throughout the day helping people and logging calls they feel a deep sense of contribution. If that same person has no calls coming in or they are not able to resolve the problems people are having they become unhappy and disengaged. Contribution may also extend beyond your own personal gain and company objectives. Many people want to see the impact their work is having on society, the environment, and the wider world.

Challenge and Connection are the fruit and vegetables of your career. You really can't get enough of them, and you certainly can't overdo them. Recognition and security are more like carbs and fat. They are delicious, satisfying, and absolutely necessary, but we don't need too much of them for optimum health and balance.

Unfortunately, these fundamental needs are in direct conflict with each other. Our drive for Recognition conflicts with our need for Connection, and our drive for Challenge conflicts with our need for Security. These conflicting needs are balanced differently for each person, so we all need to discover our own ideal balance.

CASE STUDY:

WHAT HAPPENS WHEN YOUR VALUES CLASH WITH YOUR COMPANY'S VALUES

Mandy* worked in Talent Acquisition at a large beverage and alcohol company. She was given clear goals and a path to promotion, so she knew exactly what she needed to do to achieve her career goals. She enjoyed her work and was very highly regarded at the company. Then, one day she visited a farm and realised that the company was also involved in the milk industry. She saw first-hand the company's handling of baby cows and she was outraged!

Mandy* is a strong animal rights advocate and vegan, so this discovery completely transformed her attitude to the company and her work. She felt disengaged and her enthusiasm plummeted. Her core values had been violated and she could no longer authentically pursue the goals they set for her as those goals were out of alignment with her values.

Mandy* was surprised at her sudden loss of enthusiasm for her job, because she had never realised how important the alignment of personal values was in her passion for her work. As we talked, Mandy realised that she was passionate about HR and all of the other areas of the blueprint were in alignment with her true self, but she could no longer stay at the company. As she looked at job prospects she was very careful to investigate the values of the companies she considered as she knew that she needed to believe in their overall vision and purpose if she was to promote the company to incoming talent. As she moved back into her Career Sweet Spot, all her old enthusiasm and energy were reignited.

---

*Names have been changed to protect privacy

COACHING QUESTIONS ON YOUR VALUES

- ☐ Do you feel like you are growing as much as you could?
- ☐ If not, when did you stop growing?
- ☐ What areas do you want to grow in?
- ☐ What does contribution mean to you?
- ☐ Are you contributing and making as much impact in your role as you would like?
- ☐ If not what would you like to change?
- ☐ Would you like to make more of a contribution outside your work on a social, environmental and global stage?

CHAPTER 13
YOUR INTERESTS

"Focus on what you are doing right"
- Gallup Institute

When I work with my clients, one of the first questions I ask them is 'what do you want to do?' Almost always they say 'something that interests me'. After digging into this question with thousands of people, 'interests' commonly means the combination of what makes them feel good and what they are genuinely curious about.

It has a bit to do with purpose but it's a bit more light and fluffy than that. So in this chapter we are going to focus on putting a lens on discovering what your curiosities are, identifying your strengths and thinking about what actually makes you feel good.

IDENTIFYING YOUR STRENGTHS

Now that you know what you value (your influences), it is important to know your strengths. When your career is aligned with your strengths you are far more likely to succeed in achieving your most ambitious goals.

Many modern work places have a tendency to focus on things you are not doing so well and provide a list of areas for improvement. This is largely due to the almost universal adoption of the Performance Review Process. Performance Reviews certainly have their place, and, when done well, can provide you with feedback mechanism to help you grow. However, often the conversation only focuses on your weaknesses and gaps and you end up thinking that the only way to get where you want to be in your career is to overcome those weaknesses.

However, the point of finding a career you love is discovering what you do well even though you will also need to work on your weaknesses. With this in mind, you can use your Performance Reviews to help you become more self-aware and give you an accurate assessment of your strengths and weaknesses that you will use as you go on to discover and design your Career Roadmap.

TASK

Before your review, take time to consider what is working for you.

- What are you doing well?
- What do other people say you are good at?
- Where do you excel?

This Roadmap is the fastest path to a career future that will be fulfilling. Along the way in The Roadmap we'll identify any skill and knowledge gaps so that you can work on them in order to get where you want to be, and it is important to have a strong self-awareness of your weaknesses. However, I don't recommend you make any career decisions that require you to 'be what you are not' in order to succeed. Most people go further when they build on their strengths.

CASE STUDY
FOCUSING ON YOUR STRENGTHS IN PRACTICE

When I went back to work after maternity leave I worked part time as a Business Manager for an IT Consulting company. I really wanted to take this role as I was looking for something new and different. Most aspects of the role seemed a good fit for me: account management (ultimately a sales role), relationship management (which I love), in the technology industry where I had spent the previous eight years so I had good contacts, and it involved placing people on-site in a technology delivery role which was remarkably similar to a recruitment role.

It was a great fit, except for one thing: part of my role was reading the very long, very technical documents that our consultants were putting together for a large bid at a government agency. I had to prepare, edit, and create extremely technical proposals as part of the process. Not only was I not good at this, it was a huge personality conflict for me. I am literally not wired to read long, technical documentation. I would start to read documents on Oracle environments and feel myself nodding off! This was not just a weakness, I actually felt as though my soul was slipping out of my body while I was reading these things so I was obviously out of alignment with this work.

Had I received feedback that my performance in this role was great except for my ability to write and prepare those documents I wonder what my career goals would have looked like? Perhaps I would have gone on a proposal writing course. Perhaps I would have sought mentorship from a senior staff member who was great at writing them. However, I knew that that skill was 'not who I was'. It was not how I was wired, not my strength, and I also didn't value that type of sales process. Recognising that I enjoy relationship-centric, conversational, and fast paced sales processes helped me make the decision to move back into the recruitment industry.

The Gallup Institute in the USA has interviewed over 10 million people during a 40-year study to define the 34 most common talents/strengths. Their studies indicate that people who have the opportunity to focus on their strengths every day are six times as likely to be engaged in their jobs and more than three times as likely to report having an excellent quality of life in general. The theory is that it is more effective to build on what you are naturally good at rather than trying to walk the path of most resistance.

However, many people struggle to identify exactly what they are good at and they don't know how to discover their strengths. So, here's my easy personal SWOT (Strengths, Weaknesses, Opportunities, Threats) analysis tool.

AN EASY ASSESSMENT TOOL - MINI 360 DEGREE FEEDBACK SURVEY

Have you ever watched those talent shows like 'The Voice' or 'Australian Idol'? Did you notice that they plant a few 'not so great' singers for our entertainment early in the audition process? I always wondered, "Why didn't their parents or friends tell them they just could not sing?" Not only did these candidates have no self-awareness they presumably had no feedback from the people around them. Who knows! Maybe they received feedback and chose to ignore it, and a few TV executives thought it was a great opportunity for mockery.

Either way when you are sitting down thinking about your strengths and weaknesses I recommend that you check in with people who know and care about you in order to validate your self-analysis.

A quick and easy way to do this is to send three people the same email asking them these four questions:

1. What are my strengths?

2. What are the different ways I add value?

3. What are my weaknesses?

4. How do I sabotage myself?

You can send it to more than three people but you want to ask at least one person who is your peer or works with you at the same level, one person who is a manager or works at a higher level than you, and one

Your Interests

person who is outside your work environment like a family member or friend. You will probably learn something new and encouraging about yourself! The magical part of self-awareness and seeking feedback from people around you is that you get to expand and learn things about yourself that you didn't even know existed. Welcome to uncovering parts of your pure potential!

If you are familiar with the Johari Window, there are parts of yourself that you don't yet even know exist and parts that live in a sort of blind spot to you and others. This is very exciting! The diagram over the page gives an idea of how much untapped potential you might have.

JOHARI WINDOW
KNOW YOUR STRENGHTS

	CONFIRMED	UNCONFIRMED
KNOWN	**KNOWN TO ALL** I KNOW I'M GOOD & PEOPLE TELL ME. I'VE CONFIRMED MY STRENGTH IN AN ASSESSMENT • FEEDBACK • SELF-ASESSMENT • EXTERNAL-ASESSMENT	**KNOWN TO SELF** I THINK I'M GOOD BUT NO-ONE HAS NOTICED • NO FEEDBACK • SELF-ASESSMENT • NO EXTERNAL-ASESSMENT
UNKNOWN	**UNKNOWN TO SELF** OTHERS THINK I'M GOOD & I DON'T EVEN REALISE • NO FEEDBACK • NO SELF-ASESSMENT • EXTERNAL-ASESSMENT	**UNTAPPED POTENTIAL** I DON'T KNOW IF I'M GOOD, OR I HAVN'T TRIED & OTHERS DONT KNOW • NO EXPERIENCE • NO FEEDBACK • NO EXTERNAL-ASESSMENT • NO SELF-ASESSMENT

Your Interests

In the top right quadrant you will find your confirmed strengths that many people know about. These are things that others notice or agree that you have if you point them out. They may have been identified or validated through some kind of assessment. In the top right quadrant you also have strengths which are confirmed but unknown to you. These are things that you do well without even realising that you were good at them. One of my clients told me the story of meeting with her manager. He told her how impressed he was with her ability to pull the team together and improve their processes. He wanted her to apply for a leadership role and she was floored. She didn't think of herself as a leader as she was rather shy and introverted. After looking at the evidence from several people it was clear that she did, in fact, have many strengths that made her a great leader.

One way to uncover these areas of unknown expertise is to ask others about things you are doing well, as well as things in which you can improve. You should also continue to assess yourself and take other assessments (exams, online assessments, mentoring, coaching).

The lower 2 quadrants, which address your unconfirmed strengths is the most exciting part of all. These are strengths you don't yet know about and others don't know you have. This is an area of untapped potential simply because you haven't tried things in this area yet. To help you uncover strengths in this quadrant, you need to try new things, develop new skills, speak to people who are completely outside your area and open your mind to possibilities!

The key to solving the mystery of the unknown strengths of each quadrant will be one or all of three things:

1. Validation via feedback (as discussed above in the mini 360 Degree Review)

2. Validation via self-assessment (your own observations of yourself)

3. Validation via external-assessment (online tests, performance review, mentoring, exams)

Ultimately you want to have all your strengths in the 'known to all' quadrant. This is where you know what your strengths are as they have been validated and confirmed by others.

For a free 'done for you' 360 Degree Feedback Email Script' head to my website and download a copy at *www.rachelsparkes.com.au/resources*

CASE STUDY

GETTING CLEAR ON YOUR STRENGTHS

Rhianna* is a Communications Manager in an Accounting company. When she attended a Career Development workshop, she realised that she wanted to gain a greater understanding of her strengths. Looking at the Johari Window, she created the following plan to confirm and discover her strengths:-

SELF-ASSESSMENT: She wrote down all the things that she thought she was good at.

EXTERNAL ASSESSMENT: She took an online Gallup Strengths' finder to identify her strengths, and looked at her recent university transcripts to see what subjects she scored highly in.

FEEDBACK: She wrote down the things that other people tell her she is good at; met with her manager to discuss her top strengths; and sent emails to a peer, a friend, a senior manager, a staff member, and a stakeholder to ask them what they thought her top three strengths are.

Once she had this information, she ensured that each strength that was then known by her, was also confirmed by others and validated via an external assessment.

After performing this exercise she was confident and aware of her strengths, and knew that others are also aware of these strengths.

---

*Names have been changed to protect privacy

YOUR CURIOSITIES AND INTERESTS

Interests are pretty closely related to purpose and passion but are slightly different. They can change and they are more rooted in your personality and wiring so therefore more intrinsic in nature than purpose. They are also slightly less intense in nature than passion and can be more of a slight curiosity than an all-consuming passion. That's why I like them. As long as you are a little bit curious and as long as they make you feel good - they stay.

COACHING QUESTIONS FOR YOUR INTERESTS

☐ What sorts of activities lift your spirits and feed your energy?

☐ What activities make time disappear for you?

☐ What activities are 'pure fun' for you?

☐ What subjects do you find yourself Googling or following on social media?

☐ What 'extra-curricular' groups are you part of inside your organisation?

☐ Do you have any causes, charities or quests that you are championing in your career?

☐ Do you participate in any hobbies outside of work, or would you like to start one or return to one?

☐ Are there things that you've always loved to do but not focused on fully?

☐ When do you feel that you are being most true to yourself?

☐ What are things you do that give you a burning/excited feeling in your stomach?

So, now you've dug deep into your mind and heart and discovered who you are, and what you want, it's time to go ahead and start dreaming about where you want to end up. With your Career Blueprint mapped out in front of you, it's time to move on to the nitty-gritty of designing a plan to get you from here to there. The Design-IT Quadrant is where you start to see external validation of your hard inner work.

THE DESIGN-IT QUADRANT

This quadrant is all about career design. You have found your Career Blueprint, and are clear about your sweet spot at the intersection of your Identity, Interests, and Influences. The transition from your existing position to your destination will involve deliberately designing a WAY to get there. In this quadrant you will consider both your professional development plan and your personal development plan. It's also the time to consider how you design your transition with minimal risk and financial impact, especially if you are making a complete career overhaul like changing location, industry, or starting your own business.

The Epic Career Quest is about deliberately designing your career pathway so in this quadrant we will focus on:

- Your Goals
- Your Gaps
- Your Game Plan

CHAPTER 14
YOUR GOALS

"If you don't know where you are going, you might wind up someplace else."
- Yogi Berra

HOLISTIC GOAL SETTING

When I talk about 'holistic goal setting', I'm talking about setting goals that take into account your Career Blueprint (how you are wired, what's important to you and what you are interested in), as well as your longer term career and personal goals. It also needs to take into account your current life situation so that you are not overcommitted in the present because you realise that you can fit everything into your 40+ year career.

I spoke to a woman recently who was incredibly stressed because she wanted to start an online business. She was a high achiever doing extremely well in insurance sales but she had this other goal she wanted to achieve. Then she told me she was pregnant and, while excited about her pregnancy, she was devastated because she would have to give up her dream of running that business!

No Way! Holistic goal-setting leaves you room to actually live your life. For her, all this means is that the plan for her online business is not a top priority for the next few years while she focuses on other things. It doesn't matter whether it takes 12 months or 10 years to get around to it, as long as she knows that it's in her plan for the future.

When you take a trip using your GPS, you need to decide what your destination is before you can expect the GPS to take you there. In the same way, when you think about your career you need to decide on your destination or goal first before you can determine the path you need to follow and identify any obstacles that might appear along the way. The best way to do this is to start with the end in mind. This means that you should know your long-term goal and work backwards to where you are today, rather than starting with your next steps.

In my experience working in recruitment, the best (and most successful) candidates are those who can clearly articulate how a particular job fits in with their long-term personal and professional goals. While a career can have many twists and turns, people who have some idea about their long-term destination generally feel more connected to their current role, are more driven, motivated, and more likely to seek opportunities to grow and stretch themselves over the course of their career.

THE THREE STEPS TO HOLISTIC GOAL SETTING ARE:

1. **CREATE YOUR VISION:** Sit down and think about what your Career Legacy Statement will be. One way to do this is to imagine that it's the end of your career. You are 65 years old and it's retirement speech time. What would people say about you? What message would you leave behind? What impact on the world, community or on others would you have had? What did you make, build or create? How much money did you make, save and invest? Once you write the speech you could turn it into a statement that becomes a guiding anchor to what you are trying to do in your career day-to-day and even in your career design planning from now on.

2. **ALIGN TO YOUR VALUES:** Ensure your goals align with your values. Make sure your goals give you what you need and feed into what you are interested in and good at.

3. **EMPOWER YOUR OWN VOICE**: Your career goals should align with what you want to 'say' in this lifetime. Think about what your message is and what level of impact you want to have now and in the long term. And remember to listen to your own inner voice and guidance when making your goals and decisions.

CASE STUDY

FROM MONSTER TO PEACEMAKER

One story I'm always captivated by is that of Albert Nobel. During the Second World War he was actually the owner of a munitions factory and one day there was an explosion at his factory. The papers reported that he was at the factory and had died when in fact he was safe and sound. To his astonishment he read the papers the next day proclaiming that he was dead!

But that wasn't the shocking part.

The shock was that they were calling him a monster, and a murderer and they were happy he was dead! Albert was ashamed and deeply saddened, and didn't want his legacy to be one of destruction, devastation and death.

So he started the Nobel Peace prize. He is now remembered for bringing peace to our planet instead of death and destruction. This is what a vision and Career Legacy Statement can do for your career.

So, now that you have written your goals down, and before you start designing your path towards your goals, ask yourself these questions:-

1. Are my goals in alignment with my identity?

2. Are my goals in alignment with my influences?

3. Are my goals in alignment with my interests?

If not, then now is the time to adjust your goals so that they truly reflect who you are, what you love, and the legacy you want to leave behind.

THE THREE TYPES OF GOALS

When I sit down with my clients to create goals I like them to tell me what they want. Then I get them to put them into three categories.

1. **SAFE GOALS:** Theses goals are the ones that they know they can achieve. They have probably done them before or something similar. They are not really going to push themselves.

2. **STRETCH GOALS.** These goals are as they sound, stretch goals. The individual is going to have to level up, learn, develop and stretch their current capabilities, mindsets, networks and get out of their comfort zones to get there. I like these goals and so does the individual. These goals tend to create more motivation and fire in the individual.

3. **FAITH GOALS:** My favourite goals. These are the goals that you have no freaking idea how you are going to complete. They are counter-intuitive. You set an idea, destination or number so big that it's almost impossible to achieve. What I like about these goals is that you have to have faith to get there but the key being you have to grow exponentially to become another person to step into the goal. You will require a new level of emotional, mental, physical and spiritual development to reach this goal.

CASE STUDY

FAITH GOALS

When I decided to join the Thought Leaders Business School I had a big goal. My goal was to be an international expert (speaker, author, mentor, facilitator, trainer, coach) on Career Transformation who runs a successful practice delivering career and business transformation programs both in person, online and in corporate organisations in Australia and overseas within a year. Now when I looked at this goal I was running a HR Consulting practice for technology businesses mixed with the odd IT recruitment placement here and there. Sure I had the expertise but to actually run a Thought Leadership Practice, write a book, write the programs, launch them online and sell them to individuals and corporates within a year? It was a monumental task. But it's one year on and as I write these words, I'm pleased to say that all of those things have happened for me (or I have happened to them). My international Thought Leadership Practice is up, running and thriving with clients all over the world in Australia, Canada, USA, New Zealand and the UK. With the publishing of this book my final goal in that statement has been achieved.

The physical, emotional, spiritual and mental growth and the 'version of myself' I have had to become in order to reach that goal is nothing short of miraculous. This was a faith goal so big I almost didn't believe it possible when I set it. But that's the magic of faith. It's believing in things we don't yet see but taking action anyway.

COACHING QUESTIONS FOR YOUR GOALS

☐ What are your progress goals? (Positions, payrises, promotions)

☐ What are your professional and personal development goals? (Learning, mindset, training)

☐ What are your body-mind goals? (Meditation, yoga, spirituality)

☐ What are your family goals? (Marriage, more kids)

☐ What are your giving goals? (Charity, time, stuff)

☐ What are your recreation goals? (Art, Sport, travel, fun)

☐ What are your financial goals? (Assets, investments, debt reduction, savings)

☐ What are your entrepreneurial goals? (Startup, passion project, online biz)

CHAPTER 15
YOUR GAPS

> "What I suggest is that you take charge and do the identification of the GAPS yourself. Stop asking your manager to tell you what you should do with your career and start designing your future for yourself and taking steps to make it happen."
> - Georgia Murch - Fixing Feedback

Now that you have specific goals to aim at, we'll look at the types of obstacles that you will have to face that stand between you and your goal, the things that I call GAPS. These are the unique and specific holes in your skills, personality, or thinking that stop you from stepping into your next position.

Once you dream up your goal, it's super-exciting to imagine what life will bring when you reach it. However, the reality is that immediately after you create a goal there is a GAP. There is always some kind of distance between where you are now and your desired destination (if there wasn't, it would be a present reality, not a goal!). GAPS are awesome! You want to be stretched. You want to have something to strive for, something that is going to push you and get you excited about moving forwards.

Many people wait for their managers to identify their GAPS and tell them what to do about them. However, you are on an Epic Career Quest, so you are taking responsibility for your own progress, not waiting around for someone to tell you what to do.

While obstacles can arise at any time, GAPS only appear when you have created a specific goal for yourself and you want to move towards it. Once you learn how to identify any GAPS, and work out how to close them you'll be able to prepare yourself for any positional move you want using the PRESET Test. The PRESET test tool is shown in the image below. It is easy to use and helps you define the really specific actions you need to move from career design to actually making it happen.

All you need is a piece of paper and about 30 minutes of your time.

THE 'PRESET' TEST

PEOPLE – DO YOU KNOW THE RIGHT PEOPLE WHO WILL INFLUENCE DECISIONS ABOUT YOUR NEXT STEP?

RELATIONSHIPS – DO YOU HAVE POSITIVE RELATIONSHIPS WITH THE PEOPLE WHO WILL INFLUENCE DECISIONS ON YOUR NEXT SETP?

EXPERIENCE – DO YOU HAVE THE RIGHT OR ENOUGH PRACTICAL EXPERIENCE?

SKILLS – DO YOU HAVE THE RIGHT TECHNICAL AND SOFT SKILLS?

EDUCATION – DO YOU HAVE THE RIGHT CERTIFICATIONS, EDUCATION OR QUALIFICATIONS?

THINKING – DO YOU HAVE THE RIGHT MINDSET AND BELIEFS FOR THE NEXT STEP?

Your Gaps

On a piece of paper write down at the left hand side the following letters:

P

R

E

S

E

T

Next to each of the letters answer the following questions:

PEOPLE
☐ Do you know the right people in your target organisations?

☐ Who are the people with the money, authority, and need to hire you for your next role?

☐ Who are the people who could influence a decision about hiring you for your next role?

☐ Write an exhaustive list of all such people within the organisations you are targeting. This can also include people within your current organisation who will influence your next step. It could be a handful of people, or, if you are looking at targeting an industry, it could be 50 - 150 people.

One of my recent clients in Canada wanted to move from a role as an electrical engineer in the Mining industry to the Personal Development industry. He had worked in sales before and identified that this was his path forward. He was open to relocating to California for the role, so he researched 50 companies in the leadership training and personal development area. Using LinkedIn he was then able to identify 150 specific contacts at the organisations that he was interested in working for who could assist him in his search for these roles. The first step for him was to reach out and make a connection via LinkedIn or email without asking for a job up front.

RELATIONSHIPS

- [ ] What is your current relationship with those people?
- [ ] How are you going to make contact with them before an interview?
- [ ] How are you going to tell them about what you do and why you are capable of moving to the next level?
- [ ] What is your pre-interview plan to make and keep contact with them and position yourself as the expert in that area?
- [ ] How can you do that in a way that adds value to them rather than just 'telling them what you can do' in an interview?

I have coached many people within an organisation who 'know' the key people of influence for their next step but don't really have a relationship with them. At a minimum these key people of influence should know what your future career plans are and what you are doing to position and prepare yourself to get there. That way, when the opportunity arises they will think of you, and put your name forward.

One man I knew was dumbfounded when he missed out on a senior promotion. He talked to the people of influence and learned that there were key areas of skill that he hadn't demonstrated in the interview but, in fact, he was already doing these things in his daily role. As a result, we worked on a clear positioning strategy which included communicating his plans to his people of influence along with the timing of such a move. He told them why he thought he was already prepared for such a position and where he felt he was in need of improvement as well as asking their advice on his GAPS. He also let them know about the development activity that he had committed to over the next 6-12 months and promised to update them on his progress every quarter. The next time the role was available he had almost no need to demonstrate his skill in the interview because he had already positioned himself through his prior relationship-building.

EXPERIENCE

- [ ] Do you have the right experience?
- [ ] If you don't, what can you do in your current role to gain that experience?
- [ ] How can you include it in your development plan so you can eventually have a solid example to talk about in an interview?

Your Gaps

Many times I have clients pull out a position description in a session with me and 'guess' what experience they would need to land the role. I also have them talk about where they want to move next and they still 'guess' the experience which would be required to operate at the next level or in the next role. You don't want to be 'guessing' something as important as this, you want to know!

The key to knowing, rather than guessing what is required, is to ask the people of influence, those hiring, or even someone who is in the role already, what experience they require to be successful in this role. Once your information is validated by hard facts you can assess your current skills against this information. Typically, men overestimate their skills in their application, get an interview, miss out on the position and experience a huge hit to their confidence. With women it's often the opposite, they assume they don't have the right level of the skills, and talk themselves out of applying for the role.

No great line manager expects you to be 100% competent in every single skill on the position description, they want you to have room for growth. There will be essential skills that you need, but there will also be areas of compromise and aspects that they are willing to forgo for things like an amazing attitude, proven ability to innovate, great team work, self-leadership skills, and general cultural fit. Where possible, learn from the people of influence which elements are crucial and which are merely nice-to-have when it comes to experience for that specific role.

SKILLS

☐ Do you have the right people skills?

☐ Do you have the right soft skills?

☐ Do you have the right technical skills?

There is a big difference between people skills and technical skills. Often great technical people make the mistake of moving into leadership roles when their people skills are not good enough. Yes, leadership skills can be learned just like any other skill, but if you are not interested in developing them, if the idea doesn't light you up, or energise you, then it's probably not the right path for you (or at least not now).

There are plenty of ways to grow and be successful apart from the ladder of leadership. You can focus on technical specialisation, business management, thought leadership, subject matter expertise, consulting, and, of course, entrepreneurial skills.

I recently worked with a client who was convinced that he needed to learn how to do C++ code in order to land a Front End Development role. After some discussion with people in the industry he realised that the skills he already had and enjoyed (like CSS and HTML) were sufficient for this role. For anyone who is not in technology this is like saying he's a barista who thought he needed to know how to make the bacon to get a job at the cafe, when he really only needed to be an expert at coffee grinding and milk frothing.

If you don't have a particular skill and you discover it is essential for your chosen career path, you need to decide how you will close that gap.

There are three basic ways to learn any new skill. You can:

1. Learn through experience
2. Learn through coaching
3. Learn in a classroom

Imagine you want to learn how to drive a V8 supercar. If I give you a book on how to drive the car and you read it, how equipped do you think you are to get in that car and drive it? Science says you are about 10% more equipped than you were before you read that book. Better than nothing, but not much help when you are trying to drive the car.

This is about the same as you can expect to retain through classroom training. If we forget 80-90% of what is taught in classroom training, very little behavioral change will actually occur. So, when you think about your training and development plan, do you default to classroom training of some sort? Maybe you need to think more broadly about your options.

Now, imagine that I put you in a V8 Super Car. You're on the track in your fire suit, with your helmet on and you slide into the passenger seat. In the driver's seat is six-time title winner Jamie Whincup, who is your coach. He tells you how to turn, how to put your hands on the wheel, and how to change gears. As you go round the track he talks about how to move your body and keep your eyes on the road. It's a thrilling experience for you and you are totally inspired! But, how equipped do you think you are to get in the car and drive it? Science says you're only about 20% better equipped, but it's certainly fun to learn from people who are genuine experts, and can tell us how things are done at the highest level.

But, the real magic always comes when we are in the driver's seat. So, imagine you slide behind the wheel. Feel the accelerator under your foot. Put your hands on the wheel and guide the clutch into gear. You subtly know when to let the accelerator and clutch out and when to change gear based on how the car is moving and what it needs, because you are doing it. You feel every turn and you adjust. You can brake and speed up and you learn more every moment. This is experience. Now you are equipped to remember how to drive a V8 the next time you get into one. The science says you're about 70% more equipped. Experience trumps all other learning styles but when you layer several types of learning together then you are most likely to create confidence and behavioral change that really sticks.

EDUCATION

☐ Do you have the right education, training, certification or credentials?

☐ If not, when will you study?

☐ What will you study?

☐ How long will it take?

In some roles and professions it is essential to have a particular certification. For example, you cannot practice as a lawyer without sitting the Bar exam in many countries. Accountants, engineers, and other professionals usually need particular certifications. However, there are many industries and roles where qualifications and certifications are not necessarily legal requirements. Remember that experience trumps classroom training in many cases.

After talking to many hiring managers in the technology field over more than 12 years, the biggest 'why' for getting a tertiary or post-graduate certification was mostly about two things: to show that you have the tenacity and character to stick to a long-term goal, and to close a gap for a specific skill set required to get where you want to be. The only other reason why you would bother with education is because you absolutely love the subject matter and couldn't imagine doing anything else.

When you are considering different education options it's also important to keep your career vision in mind. One of my clients was considering whether to study an MBA or do a high level Business Analysis certification. Both would be a 4-6 year commitment and quite a lot of money. The BA role made sense for where he was now, but the

MBA made more sense for where he wanted to be in the long term. Once he reconnected with his career vision and big picture values he realised that the MBA was a better fit for him, but that it was something he didn't need to start doing right away since spending time with his young family and wife were more of a priority at present.

THINKING:

- [ ] Do you have the right mindset and self-belief?
- [ ] Are you holding yourself back by thinking you are not good enough?
- [ ] Are you underestimating yourself or over estimating yourself?
- [ ] What are you doing to validate your thinking and self-confidence?

If you are scared, worried, or lack confidence then it is a real challenge to overcome obstacles. I am yet to meet a single person who has not had some sort of challenge with lack of self-belief or negative self-talk. We are all wired with the choice to see everything that happens to us in two ways in any given moment, including everything that happens in our careers. When you face any obstacle in your career, including disagreements with colleagues or bosses, feelings of uncertainty, or simple lack of enthusiasm about what you are doing, the deciding factor on how you handle these problems is the way you think about them. Some of the most inspiring, capable and successful people I know have had moments of adversity and hardship, but they were able to choose to think about those situations in a way that propelled them forward instead of keeping them stuck.

I'll give you the world's worst kept secret: everyone thinks they are not good enough, everyone struggles with self-confidence. You are not going to get more confident and then get the career of your dreams. It doesn't happen like that. What does happen is that you notice what you are saying inside your head, and decide that you will be kind to yourself from now on. You also start to notice what you say about yourself and your career aloud, and you make a conscious decision to speak only in a way that is positive and self-affirming. It really is true that what you say is what you get. And it really is true that our thoughts shape our reality!

HOW THE PRESET TEST WILL WORK FOR YOU

Working through the PRESET tool will pinpoint exactly what your GAPS are. If you are still unclear after completing this process, then you can go to your manager to ask for their input, but you should be able to get most of the information from this process yourself. The key is to be really honest and at the same time not too hard on yourself.

Once you have identified your GAPS (which could be one thing or it could be 20 things) using the PRESET tool you will write a list of what these things are, when they need to be addressed and how you will address them.

CASE STUDY:
THE PRESET TEST WORKS!

Eric* came to see me because he really wanted to move out of his customer-facing role and into a product management or project management role within the next 12 months. He was unclear about exactly what he wanted to do and he was also feeling as though it was a big stretch for him. When we went through his PRESET test together it was clear that he was further along the path toward his goal than he realised. He had already built strong relationships within the organisation and worked on multiple projects that gave him excellent examples and credibility for a future job interview.

He was also able to see that he was better suited to a Product Management role rather than a Project Management role so he was able to laser-target his positioning and learning goals. The PRESET test pinpointed the exact skills and knowledge that he needed to gain in order to nail an interview, so he enrolled in a course that specifically addressed what was happening in his company and put his hand up for secondment into a three-month innovation project which also closed a huge gap in his skill set. I caught up with him six months later to see how he was going. After a quick review to make sure he was on track with his decision around project management vs product management he was set to apply for an internal product management role.

I'm very pleased to say that he got the job! He was amazed at how effective the PRESET tool was in guiding him through the exact activities needed to get into his desired role sooner rather than later.

*Names have been changed to protect privacy

YOUR TRANSITION PLAN

This task is really simple and will give you complete clarity on where you are now, where you want to be, what is standing in your way (your GAPS), how to overcome any obstacles, and how long your transition will take.

The first thing I want you to do is to open up the Transition Plan worksheet at my website *www.rachelsparkes.com.au/resources*. Before you start, take a few minutes to watch the video on the site on how to use the Transition Plan Worksheet.

Fill out all the information in Point A: Where you are now. Then complete Point B: Where you want to go. In the gap analysis section, identify exactly what obstacles you need to overcome or what is stopping you from walking into that role today. The section below is where you commit to your action plan for training, learning, and development to close the gap on anything that you listed in the Gap Analysis. Make sure you put a time line on it so that it becomes a goal you will stick to!

CHAPTER 16
YOUR GAME PLAN

"Action without vision is only passing time, vision without action is only day dreaming but vision with action can change the world."

- Nelson Mandela

Now you know where you want to go and have clear, holistic goals that are in alignment with who you are and what you care about. Now that you have identified your gaps, it's time to create an action plan to close those gaps and get to where you want to go. There are a few tools I share with my clients to do this:

1. Your 15-Year Road Map

2. Your 12-Month Game Plan

3. The 90-Day Action Plan

THE 15-YEAR ROAD MAP

This is a tool I use with my clients to help anchor where they are going long-term and to help them 'fit in' everything they want to do. One of the major problems I hear (especially from my female clients) is that they just don't have time to do everything. So they don't do it at all. The great joy of this tool is that they can see how over the next 2 - 5 - 15 years they can map out all of the things they want to do in their career so they can get where they ultimately want to go.

The idea is very simple. Get a piece of paper and draw a line in the middle. On the left is today's date and on the right is the date 15 years from now. Enter your age today and 15 years from now. Scary stuff for many of us!

Now head over to 15 years from now. Below the line write down 'LIFE'. Enter any things you can envisage that include your spouse, how many kids you have and their ages in 15 years, how many houses you'll own, approximate mortgages - that kind of thing.

Now above the line enter 'WORK'. Brainstorm ideas of what your work life looks like in 15 years when you're at that age with that family and life. Are you working full-time? Do you own your own business? Are you in leadership? Are you an expert? What salary are you earning? What's your location?

Now take a step back and do the holistic check-in. Does what you see excite you? Is this in alignment with your goals that you set in the previous chapter? Are you playing it safe? Can you stretch yourself or even add in some faith goals? Remember this is an ideation tool, not a full-on planning tool, so nothing you write down is 'set in stone'.

Once you are happy with what that looks and feels like, step back on the line five years. Think about 'what would I need to be doing five years before this to position myself for that role or work?'. Re-enter your LIFE details to see what's realistic and possible.

Repeat the exercise another five years before (which will be five years from now). And not only ask what you need to be doing five years before to position yourself but also where you want to be in five years from now? Can you get there in 1 - 2 positional moves from your current role?

The final step is to break down the 1 - 2 positional moves from your current position to five years from now. Try it out. If you head to my website you can watch a free video on how to use this tool in more detail. *www.rachelsparkes.com.au/resources*

THE 12-MONTH GAME PLAN

Once you have all the details from your 15-Year Game Plan, Transition Plan and Goals you can put all the goals from most important to least important in one list. Sit down and only write down what you want to achieve in one year. Put the most important things at the top. You will then want to put dates on each of the goals. This becomes your 12-Month Roadmap.

THE 90-DAY ACTION PLAN

Now it's time to figure out the step-by-step actions required for each of the goals you've listed above. Choose the first section and this becomes your 90-Day Action Plan.

THE DO-IT QUADRANT

The Do-IT Quadrant is characterised by two things: targeted action to position and promote yourself and development activity. You need to think about how you can best position yourself for your next opportunity, you need to take steps to promote yourself by engaging with key people of influence and you need to engage in the development activity.

The Epic Career Quest is about taking responsibility for yourself, your results and your challenges and just getting out there and making it happen through action. So this quadrant is all about doing and will focus on:

- Your Power
- Your Positioning
- Your Promotion

CHAPTER 17
YOUR POWER

"When the whole world is silent, even one voice becomes powerful."

- Malala Yousafzai

Before we dive more deeply into these matters, I'd like to address a particular issue that I'm often asked about: self-promotion. We're all taught not to put ourselves forward too much, and females seem to especially absorb this lesson early on. When I talk about self-promotion I'm not suggesting you become pushy, boastful and brash. What I do want you to become is confident about your knowledge and skills in a particular area that interests you, aware of the value your knowledge and expertise can bring to others, and thus willing to serve others and add value by sharing your expertise. This kind of self-promotion will be welcomed in any healthy organisation.

It's important to take back your power and realise that when you are authentically yourself, doing great work and genuinely providing value you should be promoting that to people who need it. In my online courses I delve deep in to the idea of mastering the power in your career.

The best way you can access your power is to identify your limiting self-beliefs. So many of the clients I work with think things that are not true and it holds them back from creating the careers they dream of.

Next time you find yourself in a funk, take note of what you are telling yourself. Simply ask yourself - is this true? How have I validated this to be fact? Am I coming from a place of power or am I giving my power away by thinking this about myself? This simple shift can have a profound impact on your life.

H.E.A.T ACTIVITY

The other great way to be powerful and feel literally more energy is to engage in personal and professional development. Earlier in this book I spoke about studies that proved that taking breaks for development improved your well-being as well as your pay packet.

The best development activity is the one that literally gives you a physical high. I like to call it High Energy Activity Transfer Development. Usually it's a physical type of event or meeting where ideas are exchanged between people – face to face. And usually you are highly interested in the subject matter. This combination of physical contact and level of interest has a lasting effect on your serotonin and oxytocin levels and that is why you literally feel 'on a high' after these events. As a tip, head to H.E.A.T Development at least once a month to keep your 'energy tanks' on high powered at all times.

SALARY NEGOTIATION

It may seem a weird segue into salary negotiation at this point but one thing I really believe in is people getting paid what they are worth. So many of my clients are women and they are grossly underpaid for being as brilliant as their male counterparts. A survey of 31,000 people by PayScale showed that 57% of people never ask for a pay-rise! The reason given was people feel 'uncomfortable'. 31% of women are more uncomfortable at negotiating than 23% of men.

But did you know that 70% of people who earn over 150K got the raise they asked for and 75% of all people who ask for a raise get one!

So this probably means that if you just ask in the right way you will get the raise you want. The trick is how you ask. In my clients' experience the best way to ensure you get a pay rise every year is the following

1. Ask for one twice a year. Yes ask for one every six months. Why not?!

2. Ask for a reasonable increase from your base - i.e. If you are on 50K I probably wouldn't ask for a 50K rise but if you are on 150K a 10K - 20K rise is reasonable.

3. Do your research - Know what the market is paying

4. Gather evidence - Get testimonials and evidence of the work you are doing

5. Negotiate in advance - Ask them what you would have to do to ensure a pay rise in the next six months and get it in writing.

6. Negotiate off-site - A cafe away from your workplace is a good option.

ADDITIONAL PERKS TO NEGOTIATE APART FROM SALARY

Salary may seem like everything, but while it is an important factor when you're considering a job offer, there are other perks to consider. Remember that money doesn't always show itself right away. A better title now, for example, could mean an easier time getting a higher-paying job down the road. Or a gym membership (when used appropriately) could save you money on medical care in the years to come.

If you're interested in taking a new job but not thrilled about the salary that comes with it, peruse this list of other benefits that might help make up for it, and get some ideas about how to negotiate for them.

HOURS

- A shorter work week (35 hours instead of 38, working a 9 day fortnight or leaving at 4:00 every Friday)

- Flexible work hours could give you a much better work/life balance.

- More annual leave time (paid or unpaid)

- Being able to take annual leave time sooner (many people use the negotiation period to mention a 'trip that is already planned' in the first 6 months' to make sure they get the time even though they won't have accrued enough annual leave).

LOCATION

- Working from home, or another remote location sometimes

- Working from a better location within the employer's office (such as an office of your own, or a cubicle with a view).

STUFF

- A newer computer or phone

- Ergonomic chairs and mouse pads

- Gym memberships and corporate programs.

WITHIN THE JOB

- A better title

- More (or different) responsibilities

- More money, e.g. performance bonuses or share options

- A subsidy or reimbursement for your phone bill, gym membership, transportation costs, child care, or school tuition

- Picking up the tab for professional development e.g. work-related conferences, workshops, classes, or membership in a professional association.

HOW TO NEGOTIATE A 10K PAY RISE IN 10 MINUTES

When you are negotiating a pay rise and not a position change the negotiation is slightly different. The biggest mistake people make is going into a meeting and asking for a pay rise based on work they have 'already done'. Many times you will get knocked back.

The way to handle this is to have a meeting and talk about how you want a raise in six months' time. You want to discuss all the value and delivery you will do to ensure that you can ask for the pay rise at that time. Note down everything that is agreed, send it to your manager after your meeting and keep them updated on how you are tracking in those specific activities over the next six months. When you have your next meeting simply say, "Based on our meeting six months ago and the agreed activity which I have achieved, I would like to discuss the $10,000 raise that you indicated would be available to me should I meet those requirements." Now you are in a strong position to receive your request because you have demonstrated how you have earned it.

Work It Real Good - Rachel Sparkes

CHAPTER 18
YOUR POSITIONING

"Obsess about positioning"
- *Jane Anderson : Personal Branding Specialist*

Just for a moment, think about yourself as a product or as a person providing a service. Now identify the value you add and the problems you solve. These are the things you need to promote to future hiring mangers or companies. This is the core of your message. We often refer to this as 'selling' or 'marketing' yourself. Many people are aware of their need to market themselves better, either within their current organisations or for other career opportunities. However, what they really want to be doing is positioning themselves as well as marketing themselves for the greatest impact.

Often clients come to me who have been diligently 'promoting' themselves (focusing on activities to get their message out and demand attention through social media, networking, and applying for roles) but not getting the outcomes they are looking for. When we work on positioning them as the expert and take steps to ensure they are perceived as such, opportunities start to flow.

In the 'Expert to Authority Model', Matt Church and Pete Cook from Australia's Thought Leaders' Business School explain that in a standard marketing strategy or Business Value Proposition, 'Pull Effort' (referral, recommendation, and positioning) is much more effective than 'Push Effort' (sales, marketing and relationship building) when it comes to your Personal Value Proposition. My 'Position Vs Promotion' model shown below takes that concept and applies it to your career so that you can use the skill of self-promotion in order to progress your career. Marketing becomes an 'invitation to connect' rather than an effort to create interest' in a product or service. Sales is now the meeting or presentation where you 'pitch your ideas and skills', and relationships are concerned with 'building a network to share ideas and solve problems'.

The exciting thing is that all of these activities are measurable and within your control. This is likely to result in others promoting your value proposition for you.

POSITION VS PROMOTION

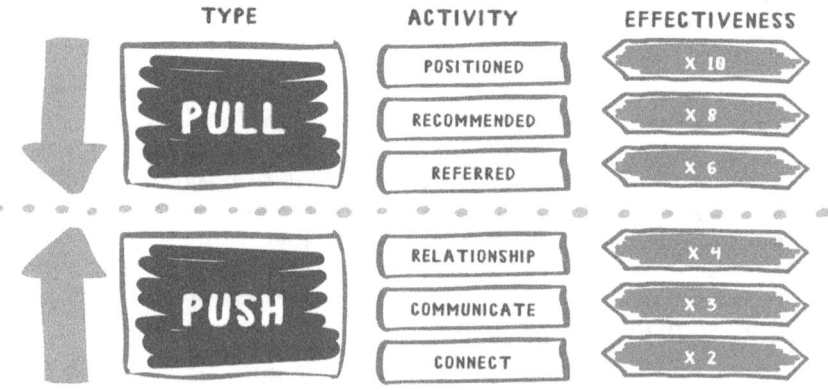

One of my clients was in a senior finance role at an online company. She had multiple large projects on her plate, managed senior stakeholders, and reported to senior managers. She received feedback that she wasn't perceived as particularly strong at strategy and she wanted to market her strategy skills better within the organisation. After taking a look at

Your Positioning

this career model she realised that she needed to position herself as an expert in strategy rather than as a generalist, suitable for any given role. That way, when she walked into her next interview she would already have established their perception of her expertise.

She developed the following action plan:-

- ☐ Identify target managers and stakeholders to connect with (Marketing);

- ☐ Reach out via email to those particular managers to arrange a meeting to discuss her idea of starting an internal group that would discuss strategic initiatives (Marketing and Self-Promotion);

- ☐ Organise monthly group strategy meetings to understand problems and suggest strategic solutions (Self-promotion / Positioning);

- ☐ Create a group page on the intranet where target managers and stakeholders could share ideas and problems relating to strategy (Relationships);

- ☐ Share her 'Strategy Tip of the Week' with this network and actively engage in discussion and answering any questions people raised in relation to Strategy (Positioning);

- ☐ Hold a Quarterly Talk on 'Strategy Lessons From the Front Line' for managers and stakeholders (Relationships).

Before long my client's managers were recommending that project leaders talk to her about their strategy problems. Then she was highly recommended for a promotion because of her strategy skills. Ultimately she positioned herself as the strategy expert in the organisation and opportunities and people were now seeking her out, rather than her seeking them!

Maybe you think that her action plan involved a lot of work with no particular end in sight, but for my client it was like building the fulcrum and lever to create momentum. She made a push effort (that is, she put herself out there and made an effort to provide great value) and, when others jumped on board with their pull efforts (they were excited about the value she provided and appreciated the benefits it brought them), it created enormous leverage and she was lifted to where she wanted to go with very little extra effort. You can apply the same strategy to your efforts, and experience the same amazing results.

THREE KEYS TO EFFECTIVE POSITIONING

We're spiraling back a bit to the Deliver-It Quadrant here, but this is very important! You need to:-

1. **GET GOOD:** Do your job well and get known for delivering, having a 'can do' attitude, and not being a dick. This is helpful no matter what. I see too many people who spend their time positioning and no time actually delivering in their role. This is going to bite you big time down the line as it affects your reputation. So, first and foremost, do a good job where you are because if you can't perform in your existing role no intelligent manager will consider you for promotion.

2. **GET KNOWN:** Decide what you want to be known for. This may not be the same as what you already do. Identify specific skills or areas you want to be known for, things that you enjoy and are willing to work towards or in over the next 2-5 years. It may be strategy, like my client, or it could be a particular subject matter expertise, or a particular skill. Once you have decided what you want to be known for, it's time to do some networking to spread that message around.

3. **GIVE VALUE:** Once you have decided what you want to be known for, it's time to identify some simple channels to consistently get the message out to your key people of influence and add value whilst doing so. Don't just cc them in on projects that promote yourself. Do things that bring tangible benefits and demonstrate commitment and consistency like running workshops for new employees that leverage your skills in that particular area or writing a blog that gives valuable advice and insight based on your own knowledge. Another idea would be to create an in-house training program that provides scalable value and positions you as the expert in that area. Your options are only limited by your interest and commitment to the outcome.

CHAPTER 19
YOUR PROMOTION

> *"I've always been in the right place and time. Of course, I steered myself there."*
>
> *- T.S. Lewis*

Along with thinking about how to best position yourself for your next opportunity, you need to take steps to promote yourself by engaging with key people of influence.

In this section we will cover all the great parts of self-promotion including

1. The Hidden Job Market
2. Networking
3. Your Elevator Pitch
4. Social Media
5. Your Audience

THE HIDDEN JOB MARKET

This market is defined as any role that has not been advertised outside the organisation. The hidden job market is real, but there is a myth that says it accounts for 80% of all job placements in Australia. It's probably more accurate to say 'unpublicised job market' rather than 'hidden' as it makes no sense for employers to hide their jobs from great talent. Perhaps 10 or 20 years ago when jobs were only advertised in print newspapers (which was very expensive) a hidden job market did exist, but with social media, online job boards, and a focus on employee branding, it's more like 20-30% of roles that are filled 'without being published or advertised'.

So, while we can safely say that there is a hidden job market, you are not deliberately being shut out. On the other hand, the best roles to apply for are those that have not yet been published or advertised. The main reason is that before a job is advertised the managers, HR, and recruiters have already gone through a process of creating a shopping list of exactly what they want. When you apply and interview for this position you are always going to be compared to their ideal shopping list. On the other hand, when you meet a hiring manager before a role becomes available they will consider you on the basis of your potential and are generally happier with a 'mostly' fit than an exact match to their shopping list.

Here is a comparison of the two main ways of discovering upcoming opportunities and can help to increase your chances of being in the right place at the right time for the right opportunity:

PUBLIC: JOB BOARDS AND COMPANY CAREERS PAGES

- Involves searching for CVs and job postings.
- When recruiters are engaged they use resume searching and job posting to source their candidates.
- Filled by matching skills listed in the job posting with those found on the resume.
- You have under 1% chance of being interviewed and hired for the role.
- Generally these opportunities represent lateral transfers for the fully-qualified people described.

HIDDEN: PEOPLE AND NETWORKING

- Involves networking and internal moves or promotions.
- Job filled based on internal promotions, referrals and recommendations.
- Candidates assessed on their past performance and future potential.
- Being referred is 50-100X more likely to result in being interviewed and hired!
- Jobs in the hidden market represent promotions, stretch jobs and career opportunities.

As you can see, the hidden (or unpublicised) job market is a much greater source of opportunity. So the idea is to make sure you are always getting in front of people and thinking about how to come across opportunities before they need someone.

YOUR ELEVATOR PITCH OR POSITIONING STATEMENT

In general most people don't like the idea of, or delivery of, an elevator pitch. So instead let's think about it as your 'positioning statement' and recognise that it is simply a brief and succinct introduction you can use at networking events or anywhere else.

I use the following formula for networking and professional introductions pretty regularly:

> Hi my name is _____. (Big smile. Warm handshake.)
>
> I am the _____TITLE _____ of _____COMPANY.
>
> I'm kind of like a _____(Analogy / Metaphor) _____.
>
> Clients commonly call me when they / the work I do helps____(Main Business Pain You Address)

Never underestimate your own uniqueness, there is no-one on the planet with the same set of skills and experience as you so don't be afraid to tell people who you are and what you do.

YOUR VIP NETWORKING PLAN

There is nothing like consistent, effective networking with strategic people to ensure that you are positioned for the next available opportunity. For high impact networking, ensure you are speaking to someone who embodies the following picture of what you want. In order to identify Highly Personalised Networking Targets you will want to consider their Vocation, Industry and Position (VIP).

From a perspective of personalised impact, the best people to network with should have the following attributes:

- **VOCATION:** They should be in the roles you aspire to in the future, or in roles you want to transition to. For example, if you are in marketing but want to move into branding you should be networking with people who are Brand Managers.

- **INDUSTRY:** They should currently work in your target industry. Determine what industry you want to work in, and ensure that your target networking contact is currently working in that industry.

- **POSITION:** They should be at your level of seniority or above. When you meet with someone who is at your level you can share information and tips and position yourself for recommendations and referrals in future. When you meet with someone who is already at a higher level you can learn from them and position yourself for future opportunities they may be able to offer.

So that you don't waste time at boring networking events take the 'Facebook approach' to networking. Facebook sends you specific advertising based on your 'personalised settings' and your networking should be strategically designed to make contact with people specifically personalised to your career settings.

CASE STUDY
IDENTIFYING VIPS

One of my clients worked in the marketing department of a bank and wanted to move into a not-for-profit. She identified 20 not-for-profit companies in her state that were the size she was looking for. She then identified all their employees who were in Marketing, Communications, Branding, or PR. Then she divided those people into groups by level: junior to her, her peers and senior.

Her initial target list had approximately 200 names on it, but only 50 of them were at her level or above. These 'Top 50' became her VIP List and she began systematically contacting and meeting them. In just three months she had made solid relationships at five different companies and had a solid understanding of what she needed to do to make the transition from the banking industry to a not-for-profit.

POSITIONING YOURSELF THROUGH NETWORKING: THE MAN PLAN

Networking is always a good idea. But for maximum impact you want to network strategically with people who have the following attributes:

THE MAN PLAN FOR IDENTIFYING MAXIMUM IMPACT NETWORKING TARGETS

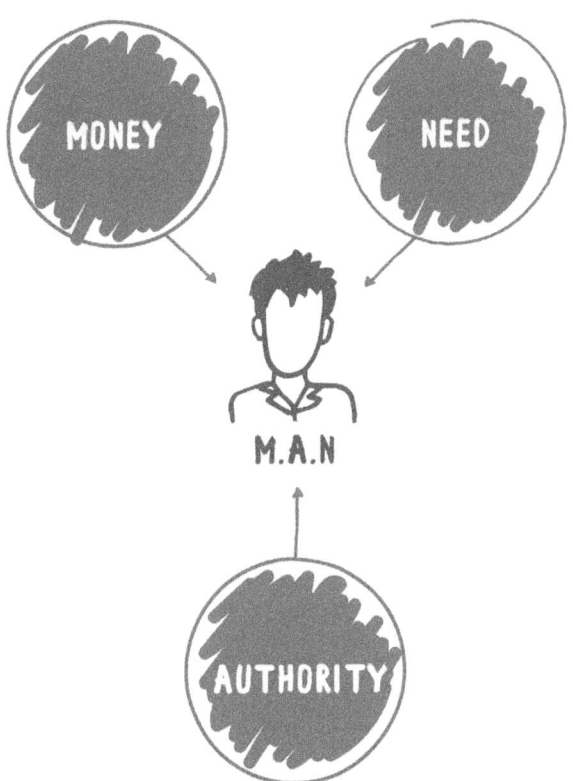

1. **MONEY:** These people have money, or access to money, to purchase your goods or services or else they control the budget to hire you now. If there is no money and no budget it doesn't matter how good you are, or how effective your solution is, you simply won't be hired. If someone indicates interest, but alludes to budget constraints then it may be a good idea to find out when they expect to have a budget allocated for this because then it's about timing.

2. **AUTHORITY:** These people should have the power to say yes! If they don't have the ability to sign the contract, your networking is not a waste of time, however, it will not have immediate impact because the decision will have to be referred to someone else.. So, if they tell you they don't have authority to hire you or buy from you, then ask who does. If they are genuinely interested they may be able to introduce you to the person with authority.

3. **NEED:** The individual should be feeling the pain of not having you or your goods and services in their team right now, or at least within a time frame that works for you.

For high impact networking, you need to speak to someone with the Money, Authority, and Need to hire you or buy your goods or services.

I'm not suggesting that you ignore people who do not have Money, Authority, and Need, because people move around and circumstances change. What I am suggesting is that you make a conscious effort to identify people who could actually purchase your product or service.

CASE STUDY

WHO'S THE MAN?

One of my clients was a Web Developer and was meeting with a new contact. After talking for about 30 minutes he learned that this person was the managing director of a small advertising agency and that he did not have any other co-owners. At that point, he knew that this contact had the authority to hire him at some point. He also learned that this person was facing many challenges with the company's personal brand and web presence, so they certainly needed someone like him. However, when they started talking about price the MD wasn't able to commit to a date over the web project. It turned out that they were going through a major IPO and all their funds were tied up for at least six months. He told the MD that he would make a note to touch base at that time, and invited him to make contact if circumstances changed.

In this case there was certainly a need, and the MD had the power to hire him, but with the company going through an IPO there was not the money for this to turn into an immediate opportunity. However, this does not mean that the MD was not a great contact and that the meeting was a waste of time, it just shows the importance of timing. The ideal person has all three characteristics, other people you meet may have none of them at present, but are still worth sharing knowledge with and assisting as best as you can. My client picked up on this and asked about other major projects that were taking up in the future.

HUNTERS VS GATHERERS

When you hunt jobs, most of the job opportunities are outside your network and your community, so you have to fight the competition to get what you want.

"People who operate as 'opportunity gatherers' rather than 'opportunity hunters' experience far greater success in their career."

When you are an opportunity gatherer, you spend your time building relationships, sharing stories, knowledge, tips and helping others grow and flourish. You treat your network as a community and care about its growth and well-being, and that community, in turn, cares about your growth and well-being. As a result, you hear about opportunities that are not publicly available and people will recommend you for roles. There is limited competition and a sense of abundance as well as a place for everyone.

Think of it like a cave man: the Hunters go out into the wilderness to look for food that will sustain them and their family. They need strength, force, the ability to think and react quickly in the face of threats and danger, and their energy and opportunity need to be constantly replenished. The Gatherers stay near the cave, working toward common goals, so opportunity comes to them.

OPPORTUNITY HUNTERS VS. GATHERERS

THE HUNTER	THE GATHERER
DON'T BUILD THEIR NETWORK	BUILD AND NARTURE THEIR NETWORK
KEEPS INFORMATION AND KNOWLEDGE TO THEMSELVES	ALWAYS SHARING AND LISTENING TO KNOWLEDGE AND INFORMATION IN THEIR NETWORK
ONLY INTERESTED IN HELPING THEMSELVES	HELPING OTHERS GROW AND FLOURISH
WILL ONLY APPLY WHEN THEY NEED A JOB	WILL KEEP AN EYE OPEN FOR OPPORTUNITIES ALWAYS
'NEED TO FIGHT' THE COMPETITION OUTSIDE OF THEIR COMMUNITY	OFTEN HAS NO COMPETITION AT ALL WHEN AN OPPORTUNITY ARISES WITHIN THEIR COMMUNITY
APPLYING VIA SEEK OR DIRECT TO COMPANIES	HAS NO NEED TO 'APPLY' FOR A ROLE AS IS GENERALLY RECOMMENDED OR REFERRED TO ROLES BEFORE THEY ARE PUBLICLY AVAILABLE
LIMITED OR NO CONTACTS OR RELATIONSHIPS	QUALITY CONTACTS AND RELATIONSHIPS OF AT LEAST 100 - 200 PEOPLE
RARELY MEETS NEW PEOPLE	MEETS AT LEAST 1 - 2 NEW PEOPLE PER MONTH
SCARCITY MENTALITY	ABUNDANCE MENTALITY
APPROXIMATELY 1% CHANCE OF LANDING A ROLE THEY ARE RECOMMEDED FOR	APPROXIMATELY 80% - 90% CHANCE OF LANDING A ROLE THEY ARE RECOMMEDED FOR

THE 100 COFFEE CHALLENGE NETWORKING STRATEGY

I hate boring networking events! It's hard to meet the people you need to talk to, so I have developed my 100 Coffee Challenge Strategy. It's simple, effective, and surprisingly productive for both myself, and my clients. All you need to do is to challenge yourself to have 100 Coffee meetings in a year with people you don't directly work with. That is just two people per week.

They can be new or existing contacts, and inside or outside your organisation. However, they need to be at your level or above. They can be in totally different industries.

Your aim is to share and receive knowledge, tips, and ideas on how to improve what you do and vice versa. Over time, these people will become your network. If you meet 100 people per year, you will never have to fear redundancy or stay in a job you don't like. You can go to your network, know where the opportunities are, and have an 80-90% chance of landing any role.

THREE-STEPS TO DOMINATING LINKEDIN FOR NETWORKING

You may be wondering, "How do you grow your network and get in front of more targeted people? In fact, how on earth will I find 100 people to have coffee with this year?"

The key is to leverage the incredible power of social media, especially LinkedIn. LinkedIn is by far the best social media tool for professional networking. With over 400 million professionals engaged on its platform daily and 49% of them being key decision makers it's the only platform that allows you to search, find, connect and build relationships with key people within your career.

So, here's a strategy I learned from my good friends Alex Pirouz and Mark Middo, who run a business called Linkfluencer. It's called the Three-Steps to LinkedIn Mastery. Head to my website for a 'mates rates' link for their online course *www.rachelsparkes.com.au/resources*

1. **PLAN:** First you map out a plan. This involves getting clear on your outcome for using LinkedIn, your client avatar, career or business objectives and then creating a profile that connects with your audience.

2. **CONNECT:** Once you have the right foundation set it's now time to start building a network of targeted contacts using the advanced search feature of LinkedIn to search, find and connect with those who fit the client avatar you created in the plan stage.

3. **PROFIT:** Now that you have built a great list of targeted contacts, it's time to turn them from simply a new connection into a meaningful relationship. The way to do this is through a series of four emails where you provide relevant and targeted content to build up trust, rapport and your expertise before promoting your offer which could be a phone call, face to face meeting etc.

According to Huffington Post in 2016 this very same strategy was rated as the most powerful B2B lead generation strategy online. I've used this strategy personally and it's incredible how many leads and opportunities I have generated for my business - much better than any other marketing strategy I've used in the past. I now also teach this strategy to individuals to open up doors for them in their own career. If you are interested in learning how to create connections and open up doors for yourself then I highly recommend downloading their FREE digital guide and a video. You can head to my website *www.rachelsparkes.com.au/resources* for the link on how to get access to 'mates rates' for their online course.

THE NDA POLICY

At the end of a great coffee catch up one day I was feeling elated after having met another fabulous new person who also happened to be the Director of some impressive IT startups, influential i n a c harity that helps educate Indigenous communities on healthy eating, and interestingly connected to the world of book publishing. We ended our chat with a sincere offering of help to each other for anything in the future and exchanged business cards.

On the way out of the coffee shop my new friend imparted some of the best business advice I have ever received. He told me that building a network or building a team was not about selling yourself to get what you want. People see straight through that. He said it's always best to be transparent, passionate and genuinely be there to serve others rather than think 'What's in it for me?' He told me he has a firm NDA Policy for his networking and business activity. I asked "What is that?" to which he replied "No Dickheads Allowed." I like it. It means not being one yourself but also not allowing any around you in the form of clients, suppliers, or advisors.

THE THREE PERSON TECHNIQUE

If you find yourself at a networking event like I used to, holding a coffee, a horrible biscuit, and hoping to God that someone will talk to you, then you are probably not going to get results out of the event. The purpose of going to these events is to make a lot of face-to-face introductions. If there is some synergy then you can follow them up via their details on a business card. At the very least you now have a warm way to then speak to them on LinkedIn.

Over and over again I've heard stories about that awkward moment at networking events when you have both introduced yourselves, asked what each other does, had a little banter, then... silence. This is the moment when you need to decide whether to move into more in-depth conversation or move on to another person. But how? How do you move on to other people without feeling rude or abandoning the other person?

I use the three-person technique for this. I walk up to a person who is on their own and introduce myself. They will usually be grateful to you for doing this since they are also there to network. Do the introductions and have a quick chat about what you both do. If there is synergy swap business cards. Immediately after doing that say, "So, I'm here to network and meet as many new people I can tonight, are you?"

They will probably say "Yes."

So you say, "I'm going to walk up to a group and introduce you to them so we can meet some more people. Are you OK with that?"

They will respond, "Of course."

Now pick out a group of three people. The number is key. Ask if you can interrupt and then introduce your new friend with their full name, job, company and what he does to the group. Then you will introduce yourself. This will take a few minutes. This makes you kind of like the concierge or host and immediately impresses people and relieves them of the need to introduce themselves to anyone.

Once you have done all the introductions and had a little bit of interaction with the wider group, you tell them that you are here to network and meet as many people as possible. Invite one of them to come with you over to a new group and do the same thing again. Then repeat. It really is a magical way to network.

KNOW YOUR AUDIENCE

When you are hunting for your dream career you will generally come across the people who are either gate keepers, screeners, or decision makers in the process. You may have to talk to one or all of these people in the hiring process and each are looking for slightly different information to satisfy their needs. It's important to remember that at this point you are on a marketing exercise so it's important to know who your target audience is and what they are looking for. There are a few groups of people you will meet, and I will outline what they are each looking for.

RECRUITERS

Recruiters are either internal or external. Internal recruiters are part of an organisation's HR department and their main motivation is to fill roles quickly. They don't spend a lot of time looking into details. What they want is the basic information required to either eliminate candidates or move them through to the next round. They are generally not technical and are predominately the administrators and coordinators of the process.

External recruiters are predominately sales people. They sell jobs to people, and people to jobs. They work for companies (not for you) and they get paid when they make a placement. Don't put all your eggs in one basket when working with recruiters. They will probably do a deeper skills and experience check than an internal recruiter as they are selling a 'premium' product to a client and are paid for their ability to match skills and requirements. Good recruiters will brief you very well on the company history, the team and project situation, as well as the company values, perks, and benefits. They should know details about your prospective salary and the personalities of the team and manager you will be working for. They should meet you face to face before an interview. If these things are not happening the recruiter is probably not the only recruiter bidding for the job.

TIPS WHEN DEALING WITH RECRUITERS:

- Build as many good relationships with recruiters over time as possible.

- Call them, but don't expect them to call you back. Follow up with an email about particular roles and restate your elevator pitch.

- Remember that they are extremely busy and generally have over 20 – 40 roles on at any one time if working with larger companies so respect their time.

- Remember they are working for companies, not for you, however, they should show you general courtesy and respect.

- Don't ask recruiters for career advice.

- They are the first level 'gate keepers' and will evaluate your CV based on errors, key words, and timing.

- Be nice and respectful to them, they have the power to recommend you or delete you.

- You will probably talk to them first time on the phone and then meet face to face. Always be polite and give them as much information as possible.

HUMAN RESOURCES DEPARTMENT

The HR manager may only get involved if there is no recruiter. The HR Manager is mostly concerned with process, policies, and ensuring that legal requirements are complied with. They will also have a good idea of your cultural fit and generally run behavioural interviews which assess the attributes of candidates they are considering.

TIPS WHEN DEALING WITH HR

- Unless they are screening applications they are usually part of the interviewing process and rather than as gatekeepers.

- They may influence the hiring decision but generally defer to the process or line manager for final decisions.

LINE MANAGERS

Line managers are generally the people you report to once you land your dream role. You will generally only meet a line manager at the first interview so this is your big opportunity to position yourself. They are the people feeling the pain of the vacancy and it is these people whom you need to impress and connect with during the interview, as they will probably make the final decision.

TIPS WHEN DEALING WITH LINE MANAGERS

- Understand the business pain they are in.

- Use the interview to address that pain and position yourself as the solution to that pain.

- Research their background and ask them strategic questions about the team, project, and business direction.

THE LINE MANAGER'S MANAGER/ BUSINESS OWNER/MANAGING DIRECTOR/CIO/ CEO/FINANCE

You will sometimes meet people 'up the line' from the line manager. The general purpose of this is to make sure you are a good fit for the team and to ensure you understand your position in relation to the overall business road map.

TIPS WHEN DEALING WITH THE BIG BOSS

- These people are generally extremely busy and want information quickly and succinctly.

- They are checking for team and cultural fit.

- Know what their strategic business goals are and talk about how your skills will help them achieve a financial result (cost savings or making money).

THE INSIDERS TRUTH ABOUT YOUR RESUME

TRUTH #1. If you are applying for a job on Seek or LinkedIn you have less than 1% chance of ever being shortlisted for that role if you rely solely on your resume.

- That's why it's important to work hard at networking, positioning yourself and uncovering the hidden job market.

- If you want to exponentially increase your chances of getting short-listed, follow up your application with a call.

- Get really good at making your 'elevator pitch' when speaking to potential employers, HR and recruiters.

- Call to tell the HR Manager why you are their next great hire, not to ask about the status of your application.

TRUTH #2. If you are applying for a job with a recruiter you don't need to send a cover letter.

Only write cover letters if:

- The job ad has specific instructions to send one.

- You are applying for university or government roles. These organisations normally require a cover letter and also provide detailed section on 'Selection Criteria' for you to submit with your application. I recommend spending a lot of time on the documents as they rely heavily on them in assessing candidates.

TRUTH #3. Your resume will either be trashed or moved to the next round of shortlisting within six seconds.

- Make sure there is a summary of all the major parts of your career.

- Include your education, skills, achievements and your career summary on the front page.

- Use pages 2-5 to provide more detail about your roles.

- State your elevator pitch right at the top of the front page.

- Include your current contact details clearly at the top of the page.

- Don't include a photo (that's what LinkedIn is for).

TRUTH #4. Most resumes will be sent, sorted, and ultimately viewed, in plain text via an Applicant Tracking System (ATS) so you need to keep that in mind when formatting your resume.

- The main purpose of a resume is to communicate your actual skills and experience in the fewest possible words.

- Resumes come in all shapes and sizes and there are many opinions about what the best structure and style is. I like to have most of your experience, education and a work summary on the first page with the details about each role on subsequent pages.

NAILING INTERVIEWS

Speaking from my experience conducting over 10,000 interviews, I can tell you that the majority of people don't like interviews and don't do well in them. The anxiety you feel in your body before walking into an interview is real and it's very normal because a lot is hanging on the outcome.

I could actually write an entire book solely on interviews but for this one I'll leave the No.1 thing that will transform your interviews - Answering behavioural questions.

FRAMING YOUR RESPONSE TO BEHAVIOURAL QUESTIONS

There are two common approaches you can use to frame your response: the STAR approach, and the STORY approach.

THE STAR APPROACH SUCKS!

STAR stands for: Situation, Task, Action, Result. In my experience of interviewing 10,000 or so people not many people can remember all that under pressure and it's half the reason they get lost in how they answer! So, just forget anything you've ever heard about it, and use the Hero Story Approach instead.

THE HERO STORY APPROACH

We all know the power of stories to engage and interest people, and interviewers are most definitely people. Every great story has a beginning, a middle, and an end, and the most absorbing stories also have a hero and a villain. Your story is no exception. You are the hero, and the problem you solve is the villain. Without exaggeration, keep in mind that the bigger the villain, the more essential the hero.

Using stories engages both the right and left hemispheres of your interviewers' brain so they can clearly see you demonstrating the behaviour or skill they are asking you about. This technique can be used for both behavioural and skills based questions.

BEGINNING - SET THE SCENE

Describe the situation, explain who was there, what company you were working for and what project you were working on. Explain what happened, providing any relevant background on how the situation occurred and introduce the big villain.

MIDDLE - YOUR HERO MOMENT

Outline the tasks you had to complete, describe your roles and responsibilities in order. Take them through your process step by step, including any steps you took and decided were not the right course of action. Detail the steps you took to resolve the situation or explain the decisions you made. Be prepared to explain the thinking behind your decisions. Most importantly set yourself up as the Hero in this story!

END - THE OUTCOME FOR YOU, THE TEAM, THE PROJECT AND THE COMPANY!

Outline the benefits or the consequences of your actions. Be prepared to explain what you learnt from the experience and try to connect it to the bigger picture. Eg. As a result of me doing X the entire company now saves $200K per year on IT repair costs

THAT STRENGTHS AND WEAKNESSES QUESTION

One thing I get asked all the time is what to respond when asked about your strengths and weaknesses. There is a right and wrong way to answer this question. Don't be cute and cheeky and say things like, "I'm a perfectionist," or "I work too hard," because it's cheesy and you're just saying it because you think it's what they want to hear.

For strengths you would say your strengths are actually the top 3 things they are looking for in the role. That is the easiest way to position yourself for the role without being too 'salesy'.

For weaknesses you would tell them about something that used to be a real weakness, but that you have overcome.

If they push and ask for something you are yet to overcome, make sure you go back to your list that you went through in your SWOT. The key there is that you took the time to identify your weaknesses and you are doing something about improving them.

HOW TO OWN YOUR NEXT INTERVIEW LIKE A BOSS!

Here are my top 3 tips:

- Answer all 3 parts of the behavioural question with your story clearly and with sufficient detail: beginning, middle, and end.

- Be specific, use the first person ('I', not 'we'), and past tense. i.e. "This one time at X company I did Y thing"

- Don't talk about what you would do, talk about what you have done.

FOLLOW UP WITH AN EMAIL

- Once you have had the interview this is a polite way to say thank you and remind them of why you are suitable for the role. Head to my website for a template on what to send your prospective new boss! *www.rachelsparkes.com.au/resources*

FOLLOW UP YOUR APPLICATION SO YOU BECOME MEMORABLE

- What has amazed me most in all my years of recruiting in IT is how few people call to follow up their application, and it's the same in other areas as well. On average, if 100 people apply for roles, fewer than five people would actually take the time to call me and confirm that I received their application. Of those five who were lucky enough to catch me on the phone, or have me call them back, only one or two would actually be able to tell me why I should consider them for the role!

- Most of those people made it into my client shortlist of 1-2 CV's so this is a pretty powerful thing to master, especially if you are using ineffective tools like Seek, and I recommend that you not only master this, but you do it as soon as you have submitted your application.

Here are a few pointers on what they did that was so impressive.

1. They took the time to really understand the job ad and what I was asking for in the ad.

2. They drew clear lines between the job ad and their capabilities.

3. They were generally enthusiastic, upbeat and friendly on the phone.

That's it, just those three simple things!!

CHAPTER 20
YOUR JOURNEY

"We are at our very best, and we are happiest, when we are fully engaged in work we enjoy on the journey toward the goal we've established for ourselves. It gives meaning to our time off and comfort to our sleep. It makes everything else in life so wonderful, so worthwhile."

- Earl Nightingale

If I've done my job you've realised that you can create a lifestyle you love, that is built around work that is deeply satisfying, meaningful, and creative, even if you are currently feeling trapped, frustrated, and miserable. Of course, you also realise that this will take some effort on your part. Nothing worthwhile happens by accident and that includes creating the lifestyle and career that makes every day feel like an achievement rather than a chore.

You can do this! The workplace is changing rapidly and there have never been so many opportunities for flexible and creative employment solutions at any time in history. You are not tied to a single location, employer, or career for your entire working life, or faced with the choice between following the rail lines or struggling to survive. If you picked up this book, and have read this far, then I know that you are the kind of person who brings incredible talent and energy to the table... the kind of person who is destined to thrive in this new economy.

Globalisation. The internet. The rise of out-sourcing and off-shoring. Uncertainty... These challenges will only threaten your happiness and security if you let them. You can choose to set your own course for a definite career goal that resonates with your personality, skills, gifts, and desires and no one will stop you except yourself. As we've discussed throughout this book, you can find opportunities in any economy if you have an open mind and a clear vision of what you want to create for yourself.

As I've mentioned, I didn't start out knowing everything I know today about creating a career that I love. I've made lots of mistakes along the way, and that's why I wrote this book... so that you would have a roadmap to guide you through the maze of creating a career that is deeply satisfying... for you! Through my own mistakes, through economic disaster and bankruptcy, through health challenges, relationship breakdowns, and the support of friends and family I've learned what really matters in life: knowing who I am, aligning to my true purpose and being willing to trust myself through the process of continuous learning and creation.

Over the past 10 years or so, I've talked with thousands of people who feel trapped and frustrated in their careers. I've talked with CEOs and HR managers who are trying to come to terms with the problems of turnover and motivation in the workplace, and I've learned a lot about how our current system of career guidance (designed for careers in the Industrial Age) is failing to provide people with an adequate understanding of the choices, opportunities, and constraints they face. It doesn't have to be this way.

CASE STUDY

TRUST YOURSELF... AND TURN YOUR DREAMS INTO REALITY

Janet* had an influential position in the Legal Department of a large corporation. It was a position she had aspired to since early in her law studies and she had planned and strategised to achieve it. Now she was asking herself every day, "Is this all there is?"

It wasn't just the long hours, the constant complaints, and the need to keep track of files and deadlines that was sapping her enthusiasm, causing friction in her relationships, and affecting her health. She'd expected all that. It was the lack of challenge and excitement. Her high 6-figure salary didn't mean much anymore because it was dissipated on things that didn't really matter to her and she didn't have the time or energy to evaluate what she really wanted.

Janet attended one of my IP3 Academy Leadership Events. At the end of the first day, she waited at the back of the crowd of people who wanted to talk to me, to ask the question, "What if changing my career means disappointing my family's hopes and dreams? I just don't know how people will react because I've always thought I was pursuing my goals, but now I realise I was just doing what I thought they expected of me."

I could see that Janet really, really wanted to know the answer to that, and I could almost feel the tension drain out of her as I said quietly, "Janet, it's your life, and your career. The chances are your family wants your happiness far more than they want your prestige."

I worked with Janet for nearly 6 months, helping her decide what she really wanted, develop a Career Blueprint, make the lifestyle changes she needed, and keep her moving forward with her plan. The hardest part was helping her discover what she, herself, really wanted because that was buried under many years of meeting people's expectations and achieving their dreams for her life!

There were so many things for her to work out and work through! She did meet a lot of opposition from her family, and she had to work through a list of fears about taking responsibility for her decisions, finances, and more.

---

*Names have been changed to protect privacy

Today, Janet loves her new career at a not-for-profit. Almost every day she goes to work with anticipation, and comes home fulfilled. She is so energetic, focused, and having so much fun that her days fly by. She has time to develop her creativity and do the things she loves. We catch up for coffee or a meal regularly and when I remind her of the first time we met she shrugs and says, "I was desperately unhappy, and hated the thought of spending the rest of my life working, but I was so afraid of change, especially the commitment to minimalise so that I had flexibility to do other things, now I can't believe I made such a fuss about it. That was awesome! But the thing I love most is having a clear picture of where my career is going, and the confidence that I have a clear compass to guide all my decisions."

WHAT WILL YOU DO NOW?

The purpose of this book is to provide you with a roadmap to help 'discover', 'design' and 'do' your own epic career. If you'd like to reach your goals faster, then an objective outsider to help you untangle your real desires, and keep you accountable for your actions is definitely beneficial and I'd be happy to help. Head to the contact details on the next page and reach out for a chat.

We've reached the end of our time together, but your journey to a more satisfying career that reflects who you are and what you care about has just begun! Thank you for letting me reach out to you through this book and share my proven path to a career you love. I'm honoured by your attention. I'd love to hear about your thoughts, questions, challenges, and successes.

I'll leave you with a poem I wrote about my journey of this career transformation...

The Other Side

I saw the other side!
It was a flash
A moment of inspired thought
A whispered idea from Source
A deep knowing at my core

I saw the other side!
And it was glorious
Standing with my hand in God's hand
My eyes bowed in reverence
My tears wiped away by the hands of angels

I saw the other side!
And was terrified
Of the journey I would have to take
The stripping away
The losing of the non-essential in me

I saw the other side!
And was filled with hope
Of true love, and Divine Love
Both physical and spiritual

I saw the other side!
And made a solemn vow
To take courageous action
To have faith
To walk forward in the valley
Of the shadow of death

Then one day
At the other side I arrived
And it was within me
And all around me
I was both everything
And nothing

Love's peace flooded my every sense
I fell to my knees
My heart burst with joy!!

And then stillness....
Breath....
Love.

LET'S TALK!

Enjoy the book and looking for more?
Interested in how we could work together?
Here's how...

JOIN MY TRIBE

First!, join my mailing list by visiting www.rachelsparkes.com.au there is a pop up form when you visit the site. Simply enter your name and email address to become a VIP INSIDER and receive my weekly Career Success Tips, RachelSparkesTV episodes and hear about special events, offers, and news that will encourage you in your journey.

JOIN OUR FACEBOOK COMMUNITY

Request to be added to our private Facebook group. Look Up *'The IP3 Academy - Members Only'* and you can network with like minded people and share your Epic Career Journey!

ONLINE COACHING PROGRAMS

If you are interested in my coaching programs head to *www.rachelsparkes.com.au/programs* to see the courses currently on offer.

SOCIAL MEDIA

To connect with me on Facebook, *https://www.facebook.com/groups/TheIP3Academy/*

To connect on LinkedIn, head to *au.linkedin.com/in/rachelsparkes*

To connect on Instagram head to *@RachelSparkes.tv*

To connect on Twitter head to *@rachelsparkestv*

To watch my YouTube Show head to my channel at *RachelSparkesTV*

MEDIA ENQUIRIES OR CORPORATE CONSULTING

For media inquiries or if you are interested in my corporate programs send me an email to *contact@rachelsparkes.com.au* to arrange a coffee or phone consultation.

DIRECT CONTACT

If you are interested in booking a free 30 minute phone Career Clarity consultation about my 1:1 coaching please book a time in my calendar that suits you by heading to *http://meetme.so/rachelsparkes*.

TO THE JOURNEY!

Rachel Sparkes

www.ingramcontent.com/pod-product-compliance
Lightning Source LLC
Chambersburg PA
CBHW060846170526
45158CB00001B/251